OLYMPIAD WORKBOOK

INTERNATIONAL ENGLISH OLYMPIAD

01 **Learning Objectives**

02 **Multiple Choice Questions**

03 **HOTS (Achievers Section)**

04 **Model Test Paper**

05 **Answer Keys and Solutions**

06 **OMR Answer Sheet**

V&S PUBLISHERS

Published by:

V&S PUBLISHERS

F-2/16, Ansari road, Daryaganj, New Delhi-110002
☎ 23240026, 23240027 • *Fax:* 011-23240028
✉ info@vspublishers.com • 🌐 www.vspublishers.com

Online Brandstore: amazon.in/vspublishers

Regional Office : Hyderabad
5-1-707/1, Brij Bhawan (Beside Central Bank of India Lane)
Bank Street, Koti, Hyderabad - 500 095
☎ 040-24737290
✉ vspublishershyd@gmail.com

Follow us on:   

BUY OUR BOOKS FROM: AMAZON FLIPKART

DISCLAIMER

While every attempt has been made to provide accurate and timely information in this book, neither the author nor the publisher assumes any responsibility for errors, unintended omissions or commissions detected therein. The author and publisher makes no representation or warranty with respect to the comprehensiveness or completeness of the contents provided.

All matters included have been simplified under professional guidance for general information only, without any warranty for applicability on an individual. Any mention of an organization or a website in the book, by way of citation or as a source of additional information, doesn't imply the endorsement of the content either by the author or the publisher. It is possible that websites cited may have changed or removed between the time of editing and publishing the book.

Results from using the expert opinion in this book will be totally dependent on individual circumstances and factors beyond the control of the author and the publisher.

It makes sense to elicit advice from well informed sources before implementing the ideas given in the book. The reader assumes full responsibility for the consequences arising out from reading this book.

For proper guidance, it is advisable to read the book under the watchful eyes of parents/guardian. The buyer of this book assumes all responsibility for the use of given materials and information.

The copyright of the entire content of this book rests with the author/publisher. Any infringement/transmission of the cover design, text or illustrations, in any form, by any means, by any entity will invite legal action and be responsible for consequences thereon.

PUBLISHER'S NOTE

V&S Publishers has carved a significant niche in the publishing industry over the last decade, having successfully published more than 1000 titles across 9 languages spanning over 50 subject categories. Being known for the quality of content, we have built a reputation of excellence and reliability. We have consistently delivered **"Value & Substance"** to our readers, through a wide range of titles across a variety of genres covering school books, fiction and non-fiction that caters to different people from every section of the society.

The **Olympiad Guidebooks for classes 1-10** across all subjects, launched almost a decade ago, under the **GEN X Imprint**, became a go-to-source for the school students in no time, owing to their invaluable and substantive content written in a guidebook pattern,.

Having successfully sold a million copies of the same and in response to demand by both students as well as shopkeepers nationwide; we now present before you our newly launched **Olympiad Workbook Series**, designed for **classes 1-10 across 4 subjects**.

The workbooks are meticulously curated by a team of experienced educators, researchers and subject matter experts, edited by professionals and peer reviewed by teachers. The team has poured its efforts and expertise into creating a crisp and concise workbook which will help and guide the students to the path of success in Olympiad exams. The **MCQs** identified will not only help in scoring top marks in Olympiads but also inculcate a sense of deeper understanding of the subject, by way of solving **HOTS** and referring to complete solutions at the end of the book.

Here we present our new release– **OLYMPIAD WORKBOOK (IEO) CLASS–3** having following features:

- ☞ Based on the latest syllabi
- ☞ MCQs with comprehensive coverage of topics
- ☞ HOTS Questions liberally included
- ☞ A dedicated chapter on logical reasoning
- ☞ Model test paper for thorough practice
- ☞ Sample OMR sheet for real time simulation

We have made sure through our best efforts, that this workbook strictly follows the latest syllabi and patterns of the Olympiad Examination.

As **V&S Publishers** continuously strive to enhance the readability and maintain the credibility of our academic publications, we seek the support of our valuable readers in influencing and enriching the lives of future generations of students.

P.S. While every care has been taken to ensure the correctness of the content, if you come across any error, howsoever minor, do not hesitate to discuss with teachers while pointing that out to us in no uncertain terms.

We wish you all the best for your exams!

DISTINCTIVE FEATURES

01 — Learning Objectives

They list the whole chapter as subtopics, helping the teachers to guide children in a step-by-step manner.

02 — Multiple Choice Questions

MCQs act as an excellent learning aid, helping you to understand and work on your mistakes.

03 — HOTS (Achievers Section)

The High Order Thinking Questions aim to help the student to solve Application-based questions and gain practical understanding of the subject.

04 — Model Test Paper

Model test paper are provided at the end of each book, which help the student to test the knowledge which they have gained after thorough reading of all chapters.

05 — Answer Key

Detailed Answer Key along with explanations aid the pupil to indentify, understand the mistakes they make during the course of Olympiad preparation.

CONTENTS

WORD POWER

LEARNING OBJECTIVES

➤ Write spellings of some common words
➤ Concept of Collocation

PRACTICE EXERCISE

I. Choose the correct spelling option and fill in the blanks:

1. It is __________ Bhowmik's idea.
   (A) completely   (B) completly
   (C) complitely   (D) completelly

2. I was thrilled to see the __________ on Zara's face.
   (A) excytement   (B) exytment
   (C) excitement   (D) exciteement

3. Have you checked the ______ in the store room?
   (A) supplys   (B) supplies
   (C) suplies   (D) supplyies

4. 'When are you ______ promoted, son?', said the father.
   (A) gating   (B) geting
   (C) getting   (D) gatting

5. Rekha is buying a new __________ today.
   (A) bicycle   (B) bycycle
   (C) bycyycle   (D) bicyycle

6. India is an __________ country.
   (A) indipendant
   (B) independant
   (C) independent
   (D) indipendent

7. One must share one's __________ to increase it.
   (A) knowledge
   (B) knowlege
   (C) nawlege
   (D) nowledge

8. What a __________ scarf Piyu is wearing!
   (A) lovlly   (B) lovly
   (C) luvly   (D) lovely

9. The Sun is ______ now. We are late.
   (A) setting   (B) seting
   (C) sitting   (D) citing

10. You must ________ in your dreams.
    (A) beliv   (B) beeleev
    (C) believe   (D) beleive

11. Dhruv was having an __________ with his mother when I called.
    (A) arguement   (B) argument
    (C) argewment   (D) rguement

12. Vimal is ________ a party on her birthday.
    (A) planneing   (B) planeing
    (C) planning   (D) planing

13. I will __________ come to your house tomorrow.
    (A) definitly   (B) defenately
    (C) definetely   (D) definitely

II. Choose the suitable homophones with the correct spellings and fill in the blanks:

14. She read the poem ________ .
    (A) alloud   (B) aloud
    (C) allowed   (D) alowed

15. I am feeling ______ sleepy to complete this lesson.
    (A) two   (B) to
    (C) too   (D) twoo

16. What colour is her ______?
    (A) hair   (B) hare
    (C) here   (D) her

17. I wonder if the ________ will stop today.
    (A) rein   (B) reign
    (C) rain   (D) ren

18. The world needs people who want ________ .
    (A) peece   (B) peice
    (C) piece   (D) peace

19. Ali was ________ some money for parking in the wrong place.
    (A) fined   (B) find
    (C) feind   (D) fynd

III. Choose the correct plural spellings and fill in the blanks:

20. Shweta is going to change the ________ of the car.
    (A) tires   (B) tyres
    (C) tyrees   (D) tyress

21. Are there any good ______ nearby?
    (A) hotels   (B) hotele
    (C) hoteles   (D) hotel

22. They are constructing three ________ behind my home.
    (A) factoryes   (B) factory
    (C) factories   (D) factorys

23. How many ______ are there in the room?
    (A) boxess   (B) boxes
    (C) boxis   (D) box

24. The cows have given birth to three ______.
    (A) calfs   (B) calve
    (C) calf   (D) calves

25. These are really nice ________ .
    (A) pitures   (B) picture
    (C) picturees   (D) pictures

IV. Choose the most suitable collocation for the following sentences:

26. Mihisha could ______ time by driving to work.
    (A) stand   (B) save
    (C) have   (D) make

27. You should ______ your bills on time.
    (A) have   (B) collect
    (C) pay   (D) allow

28. Do you ______ calm in a difficult situation?
    (A) make   (B) keep
    (C) do   (D) break

29. Your efforts can really ______ a difference.
    (A) have   (B) put
    (C) do   (D) make

30. Sayani will ______ a presentation tomorrow.
    (A) give   (B) have
    (C) bring   (D) do

I. Fill in the blanks with the correct collocation:

31. You will ________ if you stare at the Sun for too long.
    (A) Come fast   (B) Sing aloud
    (C) Go blind   (D) Save time

32. Sneha's surprise birthday party was a ____________.
    (A) Full success
    (B) Simple failure
    (C) Slight surprise
    (D) Complete success

33. I think India will become a wonderful country in the __________.
    (A) Near future   (B) Recent future
    (C) Uncertain future   (D) Recent past

34. The police arrested the ________ at their hideout.
    (A) Collection of thugs
    (B) Party of thieves
    (C) Club of thieves
    (D) Gang of thieves

35. I am ________ of my bad behavior last night.
    (A) Deeply sorry
    (B) Slightly regretting
    (C) Deeply ashamed
    (D) Terribly sorrowful

───── Darken Your Choice with HB Pencil ─────

1.	Ⓐ Ⓑ Ⓒ Ⓓ	8.	Ⓐ Ⓑ Ⓒ Ⓓ	15.	Ⓐ Ⓑ Ⓒ Ⓓ	22	Ⓐ Ⓑ Ⓒ Ⓓ	29.	Ⓐ Ⓑ Ⓒ Ⓓ
2.	Ⓐ Ⓑ Ⓒ Ⓓ	9.	Ⓐ Ⓑ Ⓒ Ⓓ	16.	Ⓐ Ⓑ Ⓒ Ⓓ	23.	Ⓐ Ⓑ Ⓒ Ⓓ	30.	Ⓐ Ⓑ Ⓒ Ⓓ
3.	Ⓐ Ⓑ Ⓒ Ⓓ	10.	Ⓐ Ⓑ Ⓒ Ⓓ	17.	Ⓐ Ⓑ Ⓒ Ⓓ	24.	Ⓐ Ⓑ Ⓒ Ⓓ	31.	Ⓐ Ⓑ Ⓒ Ⓓ
4.	Ⓐ Ⓑ Ⓒ Ⓓ	11.	Ⓐ Ⓑ Ⓒ Ⓓ	18.	Ⓐ Ⓑ Ⓒ Ⓓ	25.	Ⓐ Ⓑ Ⓒ Ⓓ	32.	Ⓐ Ⓑ Ⓒ Ⓓ
5.	Ⓐ Ⓑ Ⓒ Ⓓ	12.	Ⓐ Ⓑ Ⓒ Ⓓ	19.	Ⓐ Ⓑ Ⓒ Ⓓ	26.	Ⓐ Ⓑ Ⓒ Ⓓ	33.	Ⓐ Ⓑ Ⓒ Ⓓ
6.	Ⓐ Ⓑ Ⓒ Ⓓ	13.	Ⓐ Ⓑ Ⓒ Ⓓ	20.	Ⓐ Ⓑ Ⓒ Ⓓ	27.	Ⓐ Ⓑ Ⓒ Ⓓ	34.	Ⓐ Ⓑ Ⓒ Ⓓ
7.	Ⓐ Ⓑ Ⓒ Ⓓ	14.	Ⓐ Ⓑ Ⓒ Ⓓ	21.	Ⓐ Ⓑ Ⓒ Ⓓ	28.	Ⓐ Ⓑ Ⓒ Ⓓ	35.	Ⓐ Ⓑ Ⓒ Ⓓ

SYNONYMS AND ANTONYMS

LEARNING OBJECTIVES

➤ Synonyms
➤ Antonyms

PRACTICE EXERCISE

Direction for Question 1 to 12: Choose the correct synonyms of the words given in CAPITAL letters.

1. DELAY
   (A) Decry   (B) Postpone
   (C) Relieve   (D) Show

2. DEVELOP
   (A) Grow   (B) Ravage
   (C) Goal   (D) Barren

3. ENEMY
   (A) Inspire   (B) Attempt
   (C) Foe   (D) Spirit

4. FADE
   (A) Build   (B) Pale
   (C) Weaken   (D) Fateful

5. FAME
   (A) Violent   (B) Prohibit
   (C) Renown   (D) Make-up

6. HARD
   (A) Stern
   (B) Refuge
   (C) Dread
   (D) Bond

7. KNOWLEDGE
   (A) Apathy   (B) Stir
   (C) Learning   (D) Fair

8. DENY
   (A) Refuse   (B) Keep
   (C) Accept   (D) Allow

9. SHOW
   (A) Dull   (B) Hide
   (C) Display   (D) Real

10. ADVISE
    (A) Instruct (B) Move
    (C) Fool   (D) Warn

11. KIND
    (A) Affectionate (B) Smart
    (C) Nasty   (D) Harsh

12. GENTLE
    (A) Soft   (B) Sharp
    (C) Strong   (D) Easy

Direction for Question 13 to 30: Choose the correct Antonyms of the words given in CAPITAL letters.

13. ANGEL
    (A) Devil   (B) Disallow
    (C) Deny   (D) Small

14. ANGRY
    (A) Pleased   (B) Convict
    (C) Together   (D) Departure

15. ACTIVE
    (A) Good   (B) Passive
    (C) Ugly   (D) Depart

OLYMPIAD WORKBOOK (IEO) CLASS— 3

16. BAD
   (A) Good
   (B) Small
   (C) Ugly
   (D) Beautiful

17. BRIGHT
   (A) Forward
   (B) Sweet
   (C) Dull
   (D) Bold

18. BUY
   (A) Blunt
   (B) Sell
   (C) Create
   (D) Dry

19. DAY
   (A) Noon
   (B) Night
   (C) Dark
   (D) Light

20. EXPENSIVE
   (A) Wet
   (B) Cheap
   (C) Wise
   (D) Naughty

21. EASY
   (A) Difficult
   (B) Soft
   (C) Much
   (D) Rough

22. FREE
   (A) Lost
   (B) Found
   (C) Slave
   (D) Last

23. FRIEND
   (A) Foul
   (B) Foe
   (C) Clever
   (D) Fool

24. FIRST
   (A) Last
   (B) Second
   (C) Just
   (D) Senior

25. FAITHFUL
   (A) Kind
   (B) Cruel
   (C) Unfaithful
   (D) Unfair

26. GREAT
   (A) Small
   (B) Huge
   (C) Leisure
   (D) Light

27. GLORY
   (A) Infamy
   (B) Scatter
   (C) Innocent
   (D) Villain

28. PEACEFUL
   (A) Quiet
   (B) Loud
   (C) Loudly
   (D) Large

29. IGNORE
   (A) Attend
   (B) Blink
   (C) Avoid
   (D) Hate

30. INNOCENT
   (A) Safe
   (B) Corrupt
   (C) Adorable
   (D) Natural

Choose the right antonym for following words:

31. BANE
    (A) Boon
    (B) Win
    (C) Pardon
    (D) Give up

32. BANISH
    (A) Apology
    (B) Anger
    (C) Admit
    (D) Suffer

33. ENTREAT
    (A) Huge
    (B) Issue
    (C) Holy
    (D) Allow

34. BUILD
    (A) Destroy
    (B) Clean
    (C) Kind
    (D) Sharp

35. CLEVER
    (A) Dirty
    (B) Life
    (C) Include
    (D) Stupid

—————Darken Your Choice with HB Pencil —————

1.	Ⓐ Ⓑ Ⓒ Ⓓ	8.	Ⓐ Ⓑ Ⓒ Ⓓ	15.	Ⓐ Ⓑ Ⓒ Ⓓ	22	Ⓐ Ⓑ Ⓒ Ⓓ	29.	Ⓐ Ⓑ Ⓒ Ⓓ
2.	Ⓐ Ⓑ Ⓒ Ⓓ	9.	Ⓐ Ⓑ Ⓒ Ⓓ	16.	Ⓐ Ⓑ Ⓒ Ⓓ	23.	Ⓐ Ⓑ Ⓒ Ⓓ	30.	Ⓐ Ⓑ Ⓒ Ⓓ
3.	Ⓐ Ⓑ Ⓒ Ⓓ	10.	Ⓐ Ⓑ Ⓒ Ⓓ	17.	Ⓐ Ⓑ Ⓒ Ⓓ	24.	Ⓐ Ⓑ Ⓒ Ⓓ	31.	Ⓐ Ⓑ Ⓒ Ⓓ
4.	Ⓐ Ⓑ Ⓒ Ⓓ	11.	Ⓐ Ⓑ Ⓒ Ⓓ	18.	Ⓐ Ⓑ Ⓒ Ⓓ	25.	Ⓐ Ⓑ Ⓒ Ⓓ	32.	Ⓐ Ⓑ Ⓒ Ⓓ
5.	Ⓐ Ⓑ Ⓒ Ⓓ	12.	Ⓐ Ⓑ Ⓒ Ⓓ	19.	Ⓐ Ⓑ Ⓒ Ⓓ	26.	Ⓐ Ⓑ Ⓒ Ⓓ	33.	Ⓐ Ⓑ Ⓒ Ⓓ
6.	Ⓐ Ⓑ Ⓒ Ⓓ	13.	Ⓐ Ⓑ Ⓒ Ⓓ	20.	Ⓐ Ⓑ Ⓒ Ⓓ	27.	Ⓐ Ⓑ Ⓒ Ⓓ	34.	Ⓐ Ⓑ Ⓒ Ⓓ
7.	Ⓐ Ⓑ Ⓒ Ⓓ	14.	Ⓐ Ⓑ Ⓒ Ⓓ	21.	Ⓐ Ⓑ Ⓒ Ⓓ	28.	Ⓐ Ⓑ Ⓒ Ⓓ	35.	Ⓐ Ⓑ Ⓒ Ⓓ

GENDER AND RELATIONS

LEARNING OBJECTIVES

➤ Feminine Gender
➤ Masculine Gender
➤ Family Relations

PRACTICE EXERCISE

1. Chose the feminine or masculine gender of the word given below:

   Actor
   (A) Hero
   (B) Actress
   (C) Heroine
   (D) None of these

2. Chose the feminine or masculine gender of the word given below:

   Bachelor
   (A) Groom
   (B) Married
   (C) Bride
   (D) Spinster

3. Chose the feminine or masculine gender of the word given below:

   Bridegroom
   (A) Husband
   (B) Wife
   (C) Groom
   (D) Bride

4. Chose the feminine or masculine gender of the word given below:

   Cow
   (A) Cub
   (B) Mare
   (C) Ox/Bull
   (D) Duck

5. Chose the feminine or masculine gender of the word given below:

   Daughter
   (A) Mother
   (B) Sister
   (C) Father
   (D) Son

6. Chose the feminine or masculine gender of the word given below:

   Emperor
   (A) Queen
   (B) Prince
   (C) Princess
   (D) Empress

7. Chose the feminine or masculine gender of the word given below:

   Gentleman
   (A) Lady
   (B) Madam
   (C) Principal
   (D) Teacher

8. Chose the feminine or masculine gender of the word given below:

   God
   (A) Lord
   (B) Goddess
   (C) Male
   (D) Deity

9. Chose the feminine or masculine gender of the word given below:

   Goose
   (A) Heiress
   (B) Peahen
   (C) Oxen
   (D) Gander

10. Chose the feminine or masculine gender of the word given below:

    Governor
    (A) Governess
    (B) Governors
    (C) Govern
    (D) Governee

11. Chose the feminine or masculine gender of the word given below:

Duck

(A) Hen   (B) Drake
(C) Goose   (D) Cock

12. Chose the feminine or masculine gender of the word given below:

Landlord

(A) Landless   (B) Landowner
(C) Landlady   (D) Landsome

13. Chose the feminine or masculine gender of the word given below:

Male

(A) Girl   (B) Daughter
(C) Female   (D) Lady

14. Chose the feminine or masculine gender of the word given below:

Mare

(A) Bitch   (B) Cat
(C) Camel   (D) Horse

15. Chose the feminine or masculine gender of the word given below:

Men

(A) Female   (B) Lady
(C) Women   (D) Girl

16. Chose the feminine or masculine gender of the word given below:

Mistress

(A) Mister   (B) Master
(C) Madam   (D) Gentleman

17. Chose the feminine or masculine gender of the word given below:

Monk

(A) Nun   (B) Priest
(C) Follower   (D) None of these

18. Chose the feminine or masculine gender of the word given below:

Nephew

(A) Niece   (B) Cousin
(C) Daughter   (D) None of these

19. Chose the feminine or masculine gender of the word given below:

Tiger

(A) Panther   (B) Lion
(C) Tigress   (D) Leopard

20. Chose the feminine or masculine gender of the word given below:

Vixen

(A) Fox   (B) Horse
(C) Hen   (D) Rabbit

21. Know your relatives. Chose the right options:

Aunt's husband

(A) Father   (B) Uncle
(C) Neighbor   (D) Grandfather

22. Know your relatives. Chose the right options:

Brother's daughter

(A) Niece   (B) Sister
(C) Daughter   (D) Aunt

23. Know your relatives. Chose the right options:

Brother's son

(A) Cousin   (B) Brother
(C) Nephew   (D) Father-in-law

24. Know your relatives. Chose the right options:

Father's father

(A) Uncle
(B) Grandfather
(C) Brother-in-law
(D) Son

25. Know your relatives. Chose the right options:

Husband's sister

(A) Sister-in-law
(B) Daughter
(C) Niece
(D) Daughter-in-law

26. Know your relatives. Chose the right options:
    Mother's brother
    (A) Grandfather   (B) Cousin
    (C) Maternal uncle   (D) Father

27. Know your relatives. Chose the right options:
    Mother's mother
    (A) Sister
    (B) Mother
    (C) Aunt
    (D) Maternal grandmother

28. Know your relatives. Chose the right options:
    Uncle's daughter
    (A) Aunt
    (B) Grandmother
    (C) Sister-in-law
    (D) Cousin

29. Know your relatives. Chose the right options:
    Uncle's son
    (A) Sister   (B) Friend
    (C) Cousin   (D) Daughter

30. Know your relatives. Chose the right options:
    Wife's brother
    (A) Son-in-law   (B) Father-in-law
    (C) Uncle   (D) Brother-in-law

—Darken Your Choice with HB Pencil—

1. Ⓐ Ⓑ Ⓒ Ⓓ	7. Ⓐ Ⓑ Ⓒ Ⓓ	13. Ⓐ Ⓑ Ⓒ Ⓓ	19 Ⓐ Ⓑ Ⓒ Ⓓ	25. Ⓐ Ⓑ Ⓒ Ⓓ
2. Ⓐ Ⓑ Ⓒ Ⓓ	8. Ⓐ Ⓑ Ⓒ Ⓓ	14. Ⓐ Ⓑ Ⓒ Ⓓ	20. Ⓐ Ⓑ Ⓒ Ⓓ	26. Ⓐ Ⓑ Ⓒ Ⓓ
3. Ⓐ Ⓑ Ⓒ Ⓓ	9. Ⓐ Ⓑ Ⓒ Ⓓ	15. Ⓐ Ⓑ Ⓒ Ⓓ	21. Ⓐ Ⓑ Ⓒ Ⓓ	27. Ⓐ Ⓑ Ⓒ Ⓓ
4. Ⓐ Ⓑ Ⓒ Ⓓ	10. Ⓐ Ⓑ Ⓒ Ⓓ	16. Ⓐ Ⓑ Ⓒ Ⓓ	22. Ⓐ Ⓑ Ⓒ Ⓓ	28. Ⓐ Ⓑ Ⓒ Ⓓ
5. Ⓐ Ⓑ Ⓒ Ⓓ	11. Ⓐ Ⓑ Ⓒ Ⓓ	17. Ⓐ Ⓑ Ⓒ Ⓓ	23. Ⓐ Ⓑ Ⓒ Ⓓ	29. Ⓐ Ⓑ Ⓒ Ⓓ
6. Ⓐ Ⓑ Ⓒ Ⓓ	12. Ⓐ Ⓑ Ⓒ Ⓓ	18. Ⓐ Ⓑ Ⓒ Ⓓ	24. Ⓐ Ⓑ Ⓒ Ⓓ	30. Ⓐ Ⓑ Ⓒ Ⓓ

SINGULAR-PLURAL AND ONE WORD SUBSTITUTION

LEARNING OBJECTIVES

➤ Singular terms
➤ Plural terms
➤ One word substitution

PRACTICE EXERCISE

1. Mark the plural of the given noun:
   Buffalo
   (A) Buffalo   (B) Buffalos
   (C) Buffaloes   (D) Buffales

2. Mark the plural of the given noun:
   Calf
   (A) Calf's   (B) Calve
   (C) Calves   (D) Cow

3. Mark the plural of the given noun:
   City
   (A) City's   (B) Cities
   (C) Cities   (D) Cities

4. Mark the plural of the given noun:
   Deer
   (A) Deer's   (B) Deer
   (C) Deere's   (D) Deeres'

5. Mark the plural of the given noun:
   Echo
   (A) Echo's   (B) Echoed
   (C) Echo   (D) Echoes

6. Mark the plural of the given noun:
   Foot
   (A) Feet   (B) Foots
   (C) Foote's   (D) Foot

7. Mark the plural of the given noun:
   Gold
   (A) Golden   (B) Goldiess
   (C) Gold   (D) Goldie's

8. Mark the plural of the given noun:
   Life
   (A) Lifes   (B) Livis
   (C) Life   (D) Lives

9. Mark the plural of the given noun:
   Match
   (A) Match's   (B) Matchis
   (C) Matches   (D) Match

10. Mark the plural of the given noun:
    Mouse
    (A) Mice   (B) Mouse
    (C) Mice's   (D) All of these

11. Mark the plural of the given noun:
    News
    (A) Newness   (B) News's
    (C) Newes   (D) News

12. Mark the plural of the given noun:
    Story
    (A) Story   (B) Story?s
    (C) Stories   (D) None of these

13. Mark the plural of the given noun:
Volcano
(A) Volcano   (B) Volcanos
(C) Volcanoes   (D) All of these

14. Name the one word substitute for the following phrases:
A place where books are kept-
(A) Library   (B) Store
(C) School   (D) Staffroom

15. Name the one word substitute for the following phrases:
A place where animals and birds are kept-
(A) Forest   (B) Zoo
(C) Garden   (D) Tree

16. Name the one word substitute for the following phrases:
The art of beautiful writing by hand-
(A) Handicraft
(B) Calligraphy
(C) Hand-written
(D) Handmade

17. Name the one word substitute for the following phrases:
A doctor who treats your teeth–
(A) Pediatrician
(B) Dermatologist
(C) Dentist
(D) Ophthalmologist

18. Name the one word substitute for the following phrases:
A large group of stars–
(A) Sky
(B) Cloud
(C) Constellation
(D) Planet

19. Name the one word substitute for the following phrases:
A word which has the same spelling or pronunciation but different meanings–
(A) Antonym
(B) Homonym
(C) Opposite
(D) Synonym

20. Name the one word substitute for the following phrases:
A tank for "water-plants and fish.
(A) Aquarium   (B) Ocean
(C) Pond   (D) Jug

21. Name the one word substitute for the following phrases:
One who sees at the brighter sides of things–
(A) Pessimist
(B) Optimist
(C) Agnostic
(D) Leader

22. Name the one word substitute for the following phrases:
A place where bread and cakes are made-
(A) Factory
(B) Grocery
(C) Hotel
(D) Bakery

23. Name the one word substitute for the following phrases:
One who is unable to read or write–
(A) Illiterate
(B) Foolish
(C) Literate
(D) Lazy

24. Name the one word substitute for the following phrases:
That which cannot be eaten–
(A) Edible
(B) inedible
(C) Chewing gum
(D) Sour

25. Name the one word substitute for the following phrases:
A place where players go to play–
(A) Zoo
(B) Court
(C) Stadium
(D) Swimming-pool

26. Name the one word substitute for the following phrases:

    A list of words with meanings and explanations-
    (A) Encyclopedia
    (B) Atlas
    (C) Glossary
    (D) Autobiography

27. Name the one word substitute for the following phrases:

    One who performs magical tricks-
    (A) Sailor
    (B) Hawker
    (C) Artist
    (D) Magician

28. Name the one word substitute for the following phrases:

    One who stitches clothes-
    (A) Sailor   (B) Hawker
    (C) Tailor   (D) Manager

29. Mark the plural of the given noun:

    Roof
    (A) Roof   (B) Rooves
    (C) Roofes   (D) Roofs

30. Mark the plural of the given noun:

    Sister-in-law
    (A) Sister-in-laws   (B) Sisters-in-law
    (C) Sister's-in-law   (D) Sister-in-law's

———Darken Your Choice with HB Pencil———

1.	Ⓐ Ⓑ Ⓒ Ⓓ	7.	Ⓐ Ⓑ Ⓒ Ⓓ	13.	Ⓐ Ⓑ Ⓒ Ⓓ	19	Ⓐ Ⓑ Ⓒ Ⓓ	25.	Ⓐ Ⓑ Ⓒ Ⓓ
2.	Ⓐ Ⓑ Ⓒ Ⓓ	8.	Ⓐ Ⓑ Ⓒ Ⓓ	14.	Ⓐ Ⓑ Ⓒ Ⓓ	20.	Ⓐ Ⓑ Ⓒ Ⓓ	26.	Ⓐ Ⓑ Ⓒ Ⓓ
3.	Ⓐ Ⓑ Ⓒ Ⓓ	9.	Ⓐ Ⓑ Ⓒ Ⓓ	15.	Ⓐ Ⓑ Ⓒ Ⓓ	21.	Ⓐ Ⓑ Ⓒ Ⓓ	27.	Ⓐ Ⓑ Ⓒ Ⓓ
4.	Ⓐ Ⓑ Ⓒ Ⓓ	10.	Ⓐ Ⓑ Ⓒ Ⓓ	16.	Ⓐ Ⓑ Ⓒ Ⓓ	22.	Ⓐ Ⓑ Ⓒ Ⓓ	28.	Ⓐ Ⓑ Ⓒ Ⓓ
5.	Ⓐ Ⓑ Ⓒ Ⓓ	11.	Ⓐ Ⓑ Ⓒ Ⓓ	17.	Ⓐ Ⓑ Ⓒ Ⓓ	23.	Ⓐ Ⓑ Ⓒ Ⓓ	29.	Ⓐ Ⓑ Ⓒ Ⓓ
6.	Ⓐ Ⓑ Ⓒ Ⓓ	12.	Ⓐ Ⓑ Ⓒ Ⓓ	18.	Ⓐ Ⓑ Ⓒ Ⓓ	24.	Ⓐ Ⓑ Ⓒ Ⓓ	30.	Ⓐ Ⓑ Ⓒ Ⓓ

PROVERBS AND IDIOMS

LEARNING OBJECTIVES

➤ Idioms ➤ Phrases ➤ Proverbs

PRACTICE EXERCISE

1. **Direction:** Find out the meaning of the following phrases. "To bear up"
    (A) to hold up (B) to despair
    (C) to put up with (D) to get angry

2. **Direction:** Find out the meaning of the following phrases. "Take down"
    (A) pick (B) read
    (C) write (D) revise

3. **Direction:** Find out the meaning of the following phrases. "bring forth"
    (A) bring to light (B) buy something
    (C) call for a gift (D) bring a gift

4. **Direction:** Find out the meaning of the following phrases. "Break down"
    (A) break into small pieces
    (B) beat up
    (C) fail in something
    (D) enter a place

5. **Direction:** Find out the meaning of the following phrases. "Call for"
    (A) demand (B) buy something
    (C) call for a gift (D) cause to buy

6. **Direction:** Find out the meaning of the following phrases. "Carry out"
    (A) take away (B) burdensome
    (C) execute (D) go about

7. **Direction:** Find out the meaning of the following phrases. "Give up"
    (A) drive off
    (B) succeed
    (C) stop doing something
    (D) tie up

8. **Direction:** Find out the meaning of the following phrases. "Stand against"
    (A) object to (B) accept
    (C) deny (D) note for

9. **Direction:** Find out the meaning of the following phrases. "Get off"
    (A) move down (B) escape
    (C) move forward (D) climb down

10. **Direction:** Find out the meaning of the following phrases. "Go info"
    (A) move inside
    (B) clear out
    (C) move about
    (D) examine

11. **Direction:** Fill in the blanks by choosing the correct idiom. Sunaina was _____ when her best friend moved away.
    (A) pushed the envelope
    (B) feeling blue
    (C) under the weather
    (D) cold shoulder

12. **Direction:** Fill in the blanks by choosing the correct idiom. Anjali was suffering from fever. She was feeling ______.
    (A) feeling blue
    (B) cold shoulder
    (C) under the weather
    (D) down to earth

13. **Direction:** Fill in the blanks by choosing the correct idiom. Preeti did not speak to Shivangi. She gave her ______.
    (A) early bird
    (B) hit the hay
    (C) pushed the envelope
    (D) cold shoulder

14. **Direction:** Fill in the blanks by choosing the correct idiom. Ashu is a simple and ______ person.
    (A) shrewd
    (B) down to earth
    (C) practical
    (D) bang on

15. **Direction:** Fill in the blanks by choosing the correct idiom. Neeraj wanted to make quick profits, so he took a ______.
    (A) envelope   (B) apple
    (C) big step   (D) cold shoulder

16. **Direction:** Read the given situations. Choose the most appropriate idiom or proverb which matches with the situation. I thought Aditya would be a good worker, but it turns out that he can't cut the mustard.
    (A) He is not good in cooking.
    (B) He does not know how to collect mustard.
    (C) He cannot deal with problems and difficulties.
    (D) None of the above.

17. **Direction:** Read the given situations. Choose the most appropriate idiom or proverb which matches with the situation. Nishi decided that she would go out on a limb and ask Satyam to the annual dance competition.
    (A) Nishi will take a risk.
    (B) Nishi will fight.
    (C) Nishi will take some vehicle.
    (D) Nishi will go out of the way to ask him.

18. **Direction:** Read the given situations. Choose the most appropriate idiom or proverb which matches with the situation. Milind thought his mom would let him go to the party, but no dice.
    (A) There was no vehicle to go.
    (B) There was no money.
    (C) Mom was not available.
    (D) Mom denied and there was no possibility.

19. **Direction:** Read the given situations. Choose the most appropriate idiom or proverb which matches with the situation. Rohit was too tired to finish the assignment, so he decided to hit the hay.
    (A) He prepared to go for sleep.
    (B) He postponed his assignment for the next day.
    (C) He thought it was useless to do the work.
    (D) None of the above.

20. **Direction:** Read the given situations. Choose the most appropriate idiom or proverb which matches with the situation. Anurag was excited when he found out that he would have his own fiat given by his company. It was just the icing on the cake.
    (A) The flat was small but good.
    (B) The flat was beautiful.
    (C) The flat was an additional benefit to the salary he was getting.
    (D) Both (B) and (C)

Some proverbs/idioms are given below together with their meanings. Choose the correct meaning of proverb/idiom, If there is no correct meaning given, E (i.e.) 'None of these' will be the answer.

21. To make clean breast of
    (A) To gain prominence
    (C) To praise oneself
    (C) To confess without of reserve
    (D) To destroy before it blooms
    (E) None of these

22. To keeps one's temper
    (A) To become hungry
    (B) To be in good mood
    (C) To preserve ones energy
    (D) To be aloof from
    (E) None of these

23. To catch a tartar
    (A) To trap wanted criminal with great difficulty
    (b) To catch a dangerous person
    (c) To meet with disaster
    (d) To deal with a person who is more than one's match
    (E) None of these

24. To drive home
    (A) To find one's roots
    (B) To return to place of rest
    (C) Back to original position
    (D) To emphasise
    (E) None of these

25. To have an axe to grind
    (A) A private end to serve
    (B) To fail to arouse interest
    (C) To have no result
    (D) To work for both sides
    (E) None of these

—Darken Your Choice with HB Pencil—

1.	Ⓐ Ⓑ Ⓒ Ⓓ	6.	Ⓐ Ⓑ Ⓒ Ⓓ	11.	Ⓐ Ⓑ Ⓒ Ⓓ	16	Ⓐ Ⓑ Ⓒ Ⓓ	21.	Ⓐ Ⓑ Ⓒ Ⓓ
2.	Ⓐ Ⓑ Ⓒ Ⓓ	7.	Ⓐ Ⓑ Ⓒ Ⓓ	12.	Ⓐ Ⓑ Ⓒ Ⓓ	17.	Ⓐ Ⓑ Ⓒ Ⓓ	22.	Ⓐ Ⓑ Ⓒ Ⓓ
3.	Ⓐ Ⓑ Ⓒ Ⓓ	8.	Ⓐ Ⓑ Ⓒ Ⓓ	13.	Ⓐ Ⓑ Ⓒ Ⓓ	18.	Ⓐ Ⓑ Ⓒ Ⓓ	23.	Ⓐ Ⓑ Ⓒ Ⓓ
4.	Ⓐ Ⓑ Ⓒ Ⓓ	9.	Ⓐ Ⓑ Ⓒ Ⓓ	14.	Ⓐ Ⓑ Ⓒ Ⓓ	19.	Ⓐ Ⓑ Ⓒ Ⓓ	24.	Ⓐ Ⓑ Ⓒ Ⓓ
5.	Ⓐ Ⓑ Ⓒ Ⓓ	10.	Ⓐ Ⓑ Ⓒ Ⓓ	15.	Ⓐ Ⓑ Ⓒ Ⓓ	20.	Ⓐ Ⓑ Ⓒ Ⓓ	25.	Ⓐ Ⓑ Ⓒ Ⓓ

NOUNS AND PRONOUNS

LEARNING OBJECTIVES

➤ Nouns and their types
➤ Pronouns and their types

PRACTICE EXERCISE

I. Pick the odd noun out:

1. Tree, knife, aeroplane, Mr. Das
    (A) tree   (B) knife
    (C) aeroplane   (D) Mr. Das

II. Identify the common nouns in the given sentences:

2. The teacher is reading a book.
    (A) teacher, book
    (B) is reading
    (C) The
    (D) a

3. She ate the sandwich quickly.
    (A) She
    (B) ate
    (C) sandwich
    (D) quickly

4. The bicycle belongs to me.
    (A) The   (B) bicycle
    (C) belongs   (D) me

5. The sky is filled with stars.
    (A) sky, stars   (B) The, with
    (C) is, stars   (D) filled, sky

6. The fly is sitting on the cake.
    (A) fly, cake   (B) sitting, fly
    (C) on, cake   (D) the, on

7. We climbed the hill.
    (A) We   (B) hill
    (C) the   (D) climbed

8. The butterfly is a beautiful insect.
    (A) beautiful, insect
    (B) butterfly, insect
    (C) butterfly, beautiful
    (D) the butterfly

9. The chef is making soup.
    (A) The   (B) chef, soup
    (C) is making   (D) chef, the

10. The tomatoes are in the basket.
    (A) tomatoes, are   (B) basket, in
    (C) tomatoes, basket (D) in

11. She is writing a book on the Taj Mahal.
    (A) Taj Mahal   (B) book
    (C) is writing   (D) she

12. There is no water in the jug.
    (A) There, water   (B) water, jug
    (C) There, in   (D) water, there

13. The rabbit came out of the hat.
    (A) rabbit, hat   (B) came, rabbit
    (C) came, hat   (D) came

III. **Choose the type of underlined nouns in the given sentences:**

14. The <u>princess</u> is marrying the prince tomorrow.
    (A) Proper noun
    (B) Common noun
    (C) Abstract noun
    (D) Collective noun

15. <u>Ted</u> is very happy at his new office.
    (A) Proper noun
    (B) Common noun
    (C) Abstract noun
    (D) Collective noun

IV. **Choose the correct pronoun from the options and fill in the blanks:**

16. I will call _______ tomorrow.
    (A) they   (B) he
    (C) them   (D) us

17. __________ is your class teacher?
    (A) these   (B) who
    (C) that   (D) those

18. _____ am ten years old.
    (A) she   (B) you
    (C) they   (D) I

19. _________ pencil is this?
    (A) whose   (B) whom
    (C) who   (D) these

20. _______ will get late for the party.
    (A) us   (B) we
    (C) them   (D) who

21. They have invited _______ to dinner.
    (A) I   (B) we
    (C) us   (D) these

22. _________ is the house that I want to buy.
    (A) this   (B) these
    (C) where   (D) whose

23. She looked at _________ in the mirror.
    (A) myself   (B) herself
    (C) yourself   (D) oneself

24. The keys belong to her. They are _______.
    (A) mine   (B) hers
    (C) yours   (D) theirs

25. Where are _______ going?
    (A) this   (B) she
    (C) us   (D) you

V. **Pick the odd pronoun out:**

26. I, She, Me, You
    (A) I   (B) she
    (C) me   (D) you

27. Myself, Him, Himself, Yourself
    (A) myself   (B) him
    (C) himself   (D) yourself

28. Mine, This, That, Those
    (A) mine   (B) this
    (C) that   (D) those

29. Yours, Theirs, His, Her
    (A) yours   (B) theirs
    (C) his   (D) her

30. Who, They, Whom, Whose
    (A) who   (B) they
    (C) whom   (D) whose

HOTS (ACHIEVERS SECTION)

Choose the kind of noun that has been underlined from the given options:

31. Ram was sitting on the <u>carpet</u>.
    (A) Proper Noun
    (B) Common Noun
    (C) Abstract Noun
    (D) Collective noun

32. Sita drove her <u>Audi</u> back home.
    (A) Proper Noun
    (B) Common Noun
    (C) Abstract Noun
    (D) Collective noun

33. <u>Fear</u> is a basic emotion.
   (A) Proper Noun
   (B) Concrete Noun
   (C) Abstract Noun
   (D) Collective noun

Select the type of pronouns that have been underlined from the given options:

34. I didn't hurt the man. The fault is all <u>yours</u>.
   (A) Personal, Possessive
   (B) Interrogative, Reflexive
   (C) Demonstrative, Personal
   (D) Interrogative, Possessive

35. He is an old friend of <u>mine</u>. <u>These</u> are his children.
   (A) Possessive, Interrogative
   (B) Interrogative, Reflexive
   (C) Demonstrative, Personal
   (D) Possessive, Demonstrative

---

1. Ⓐ Ⓑ Ⓒ Ⓓ	8. Ⓐ Ⓑ Ⓒ Ⓓ	15. Ⓐ Ⓑ Ⓒ Ⓓ	22 Ⓐ Ⓑ Ⓒ Ⓓ	29. Ⓐ Ⓑ Ⓒ Ⓓ
2. Ⓐ Ⓑ Ⓒ Ⓓ	9. Ⓐ Ⓑ Ⓒ Ⓓ	16. Ⓐ Ⓑ Ⓒ Ⓓ	23. Ⓐ Ⓑ Ⓒ Ⓓ	30. Ⓐ Ⓑ Ⓒ Ⓓ
3. Ⓐ Ⓑ Ⓒ Ⓓ	10. Ⓐ Ⓑ Ⓒ Ⓓ	17. Ⓐ Ⓑ Ⓒ Ⓓ	24. Ⓐ Ⓑ Ⓒ Ⓓ	31. Ⓐ Ⓑ Ⓒ Ⓓ
4. Ⓐ Ⓑ Ⓒ Ⓓ	11. Ⓐ Ⓑ Ⓒ Ⓓ	18. Ⓐ Ⓑ Ⓒ Ⓓ	25. Ⓐ Ⓑ Ⓒ Ⓓ	32. Ⓐ Ⓑ Ⓒ Ⓓ
5. Ⓐ Ⓑ Ⓒ Ⓓ	12. Ⓐ Ⓑ Ⓒ Ⓓ	19. Ⓐ Ⓑ Ⓒ Ⓓ	26. Ⓐ Ⓑ Ⓒ Ⓓ	33. Ⓐ Ⓑ Ⓒ Ⓓ
6. Ⓐ Ⓑ Ⓒ Ⓓ	13. Ⓐ Ⓑ Ⓒ Ⓓ	20. Ⓐ Ⓑ Ⓒ Ⓓ	27. Ⓐ Ⓑ Ⓒ Ⓓ	34. Ⓐ Ⓑ Ⓒ Ⓓ
7. Ⓐ Ⓑ Ⓒ Ⓓ	14. Ⓐ Ⓑ Ⓒ Ⓓ	21. Ⓐ Ⓑ Ⓒ Ⓓ	28. Ⓐ Ⓑ Ⓒ Ⓓ	35. Ⓐ Ⓑ Ⓒ Ⓓ

OLYMPIAD WORKBOOK (IEO) CLASS— 3

VERBS AND ADVERBS

LEARNING OBJECTIVES

➤ Verbs and their different types
➤ Modal verbs
➤ Adverbs and its types

PRACTICE EXERCISE

I. Choose the correct option to fill in the blanks:

1. If I ask him the answer tomorrow, will he ______________
   (A) fly   (B) run
   (C) sow   (D) know

2. When he picked up the stick from the ground, it was badly ______________
   (A) write   (B) buy
   (C) bent   (D) caught

3. As soon as I went near the little bird, it ______________ away.
   (A) flew   (B) drew
   (C) sew   (D) drank

4. 'Where are you? We are all waiting for you to ______________ the cake.'
   (A) lay   (B) lent
   (C) cut   (D) read

5. Where should I apply if I have ______________ my ID?
   (A) brought   (B) sent
   (C) caught   (D) lost

6. I have just ______________ my old car.
   (A) told   (B) sold
   (C) mould   (D) fold

7. I know Mr. Mukherjee, he ______________ my son last year.
   (A) flew   (B) sent
   (C) taught   (D) brought

8. I will meet Aman today. I ______________ Suruchi yesterday.
   (A) set   (B) read
   (C) leapt   (D) met

9. Mansi ______________ a beautiful song at the function last week.
   (A) drank   (B) sang
   (C) rang   (D) sank

10. I didn't know that she ______________ her things when she came yesterday.
    (A) took
    (B) drank
    (C) sang
    (D) flew

11. She repeated the lesson and asked if we ______________ it.
    (A) sank   (B) brought
    (C) understood   (D) caught

12. It was a pleasant day so we all ______________ to the beach yesterday.
    (A) ran   (B) buy
    (C) wrote   (D) went

13. Last year when I __________ the Taj, I __________ it was beautiful. I still do.
(A) went, thought
(B) thought, drank
(C) saw, thought
(D) wrote, bought

14. Neha __________ a pink dress for her wedding.
(A) spent   (B) wore
(C) thought   (D) read

15. We all __________ up when we saw the teacher entering the classroom.
(A) spent   (B) wrote
(C) stood   (D) brought

16. Mother knocked on the door at 1 pm. They were __________ sleeping!
(A) quietly   (B) still
(C) very   (D) too

17. We came to the function even last year. It is organized __________
(A) annually   (B) quickly
(C) always   (D) slowly

18. Have you kept my watch __________? I am not able to find it!
(A) always   (B) often
(C) somewhere   (D) here

19. Rohit is very religious. He prays __________.
(A) rarely   (B) daily
(C) above   (D) quickly

20. I am not surprised that she won the scholarship. She is __________ intelligent.
(A) beautifully (B) nearly
(C) sadly   (D) so

21. __________ cross the road from the zebra crossing.
(A) Always   (B) Here
(C) Beside   (D) Often

22. I have been sitting near the phone all day! He hasn't called __________.
(A) below   (B) often
(C) yet   (D) already

23. She painted the scene __________. I am speechless!
(A) restlessly (B) beautifully
(C) often   (D) here

24. My grandmother has been ill for the last three months, so we go to meet her __________.
(A) under   (B) happily
(C) often   (D) never

25. The weather was great __________. We played in the park all day.
(A) yesterday   (B) often
(C) intently   (D) too

26. The class was __________ full, so we started the lecture.
(A) twice   (B) above
(C) quietly   (D) nearly

27. I have already watched this movie once but I don't mind watching it __________.
(A) inside   (B) again
(C) always   (D) soon

28. Nisha is a good dancer. She practices __________.
(A) really   (B) often
(C) everyday   (D) sometimes

29. Put the cat __________ the blanket.
(A) under   (B) below
(C) again   (D) yet

30. I asked her if she had visited the Red Fort __________ but she told me that this was her first visit.
(A) after   (B) inside
(C) before   (D) tomorrow

31. Match the following:

	List I		List II
(a)	she comes from	1.	my own free will.
(b)	he feels sorry	2.	the same story.
(c)	they all tell	3.	for his faults.
(d)	I do it of	4.	a good family.

(A) (a)-1   (b)-2   (c)-3   (d)-4
(B) (a)-4   (b)-3   (c)-2   (d)-1
(C) (a)-2   (b)-4   (c)-1   (d)-3
(D) (a)-3   (b)-2   (c)-4   (d)-1

32. Read the statements carefully and choose the correct option.
    (i) The sun shines brightly. (transitive)
    (ii) The policeman blew his whistle. (transitive)
    (iii) The cat sleeps on the rug. (intransitive)
    (iv) The fire burns dimly. (intransitive)
    (A) (i) and (ii) are correct
    (B) (ii) and (iii) are correct
    (C) (ii) and (iv) are correct
    (D) (i) and (iii) are correct

33. Which of these pictures suggests the verb 'swinging'?

(i)    (ii) 

(iii)    (iv) 

(A) (iv)   (B) (iii)
(C) (ii)   (D) (i)

34. The Government should immediately take action in this matter. Here the adverb is _________.
    (A) the Government   (B) immediately
    (C) take   (D) this matter

35. I usually watch movies on every Sunday. Here the adverb is _________.
    (A) usually   (B) movies
    (C) Sunday   (D) none of these

―Darken Your Choice with HB Pencil―

1.	Ⓐ Ⓑ Ⓒ Ⓓ	8.	Ⓐ Ⓑ Ⓒ Ⓓ	15.	Ⓐ Ⓑ Ⓒ Ⓓ	22	Ⓐ Ⓑ Ⓒ Ⓓ	29.	Ⓐ Ⓑ Ⓒ Ⓓ
2.	Ⓐ Ⓑ Ⓒ Ⓓ	9.	Ⓐ Ⓑ Ⓒ Ⓓ	16.	Ⓐ Ⓑ Ⓒ Ⓓ	23.	Ⓐ Ⓑ Ⓒ Ⓓ	30.	Ⓐ Ⓑ Ⓒ Ⓓ
3.	Ⓐ Ⓑ Ⓒ Ⓓ	10.	Ⓐ Ⓑ Ⓒ Ⓓ	17.	Ⓐ Ⓑ Ⓒ Ⓓ	24.	Ⓐ Ⓑ Ⓒ Ⓓ	31.	Ⓐ Ⓑ Ⓒ Ⓓ
4.	Ⓐ Ⓑ Ⓒ Ⓓ	11.	Ⓐ Ⓑ Ⓒ Ⓓ	18.	Ⓐ Ⓑ Ⓒ Ⓓ	25.	Ⓐ Ⓑ Ⓒ Ⓓ	32.	Ⓐ Ⓑ Ⓒ Ⓓ
5.	Ⓐ Ⓑ Ⓒ Ⓓ	12.	Ⓐ Ⓑ Ⓒ Ⓓ	19.	Ⓐ Ⓑ Ⓒ Ⓓ	26.	Ⓐ Ⓑ Ⓒ Ⓓ	33.	Ⓐ Ⓑ Ⓒ Ⓓ
6.	Ⓐ Ⓑ Ⓒ Ⓓ	13.	Ⓐ Ⓑ Ⓒ Ⓓ	20.	Ⓐ Ⓑ Ⓒ Ⓓ	27.	Ⓐ Ⓑ Ⓒ Ⓓ	34.	Ⓐ Ⓑ Ⓒ Ⓓ
7.	Ⓐ Ⓑ Ⓒ Ⓓ	14.	Ⓐ Ⓑ Ⓒ Ⓓ	21.	Ⓐ Ⓑ Ⓒ Ⓓ	28.	Ⓐ Ⓑ Ⓒ Ⓓ	35.	Ⓐ Ⓑ Ⓒ Ⓓ

ADJECTIVES AND CONJUNCTIONS

➤ Different types of adjectives   ➤ Usage of Conjunctions

PRACTICE EXERCISE

I. Fill in the blanks with the correct option.

1. Can I play with your _____ toy?
   (A) new   (B) brave
   (C) exhausted   (D) stale

2. The elephant is _______ than the cow.
   (A) biggest   (B) big
   (C) more big   (D) bigger

3. Do you have _____ labour?
   (A) ten   (B) clever
   (C) sufficient   (D) blue

4. Mr. Kapoor is a _____ person
   (A) humble   (B) two
   (C) some   (D) whole

5. Do you drink_____ water?
   (A) clean   (B) tasty
   (C) wise   (D) pink

6. Why are you eating __________ mangoes?
   (A) sour   (B) careful
   (C) low   (D) tough

7. Khali is a _____ wrestler.
   (A) sorrow   (B) indian
   (C) tough   (D) interesting

8. It was a _____ scene.
   (A) tall   (B) black
   (C) major   (D) beautiful

9. These cats are of ___________ colours.
   (A) each
   (B) brown and white
   (C) all
   (D) none of these

10. My friend was sitting in the_______ row.
    (A) fifth   (B) deep
    (C) bright   (D) many

11. The entire area was ____
    (A) bright   (B) peaceful
    (C) powerful   (D) tender

12. They are _____ swimmers.
    (A) high   (B) low
    (C) bright   (D) good

13. My new cricket kit is the _____ gift from my parents.
    (A) most wonderful
    (B) wonder fullest
    (C) more wonderful
    (D) wonderful

14. Manak is the _____ kid in the class.
    (A) funny   (B) more funny
    (C) funnier   (D) funniest

15. As ________ as sugar.
    (A) bitter   (B) sour
    (C) salty   (D) sweet

16. We can either buy a shirt _____ a T-shirt for his birthday.
    (A) and   (B) but
    (C) or   (D) so

17. The elephant has long ears _______ a short tail.
    (A) if   (B) or
    (C) but   (D) and
18. I got a book _______ gave it to my sister.
    (A) than   (B) so
    (C) and   (D) but
19. Is that dress blue _______ pink?
    (A) for   (B) but
    (C) and   (D) or
20. We won the match _______ we played well.
    (A) because   (B) if
    (C) but   (D) so
21. My grandfather likes summer _______ hates winter.
    (A) if   (B) but
    (C) because   (D) or
22. A parrot can talk _______ it cannot draw.
    (A) and   (B) but
    (C) or   (D) because
23. A hen eats grains _______ worms.
    (A) and   (B) but
    (C) or   (D) as
24. We were tired _______ we could not read.
    (A) because   (B) and
    (C) so   (D) of
25. It has been a long time _______ we saw him.
    (A) before   (B) since
    (C) because   (D) as
26. She is intelligent _______ lazy.
    (A) and   (B) but
    (C) so   (D) or
27. ___ in Baroda, he learnt painting.
    (A) Since   (B) While
    (C) As   (D) Because
28. Do it now _______ you will forget.
    (A) or   (B) and
    (C) before   (D) since
29. Why is he dressed _______ a woman?
    (A) before   (B) after
    (C) as   (D) if
30. Will you have a mango shake _______ banana shake?
    (A) and
    (B) if
    (C) or
    (D) because

31. Who took the final decision in this matter? Here the adjective is __________.
    (A) final
    (B) decision
    (C) matter
    (D) none of these

32. You have to be quick to catch the ball. Here the adjective is __________.
    (A) you
    (B) quick
    (C) catch
    (D) the ball

33. It was an impossible task for me. Here the adjective is __________.
    (A) it
    (B) task
    (C) impossible
    (D) me

Direction: Complete the following passage with the help of the right conjunction given below.

The rabbit has long ears __ (34) __ a short tail. It does not move __ (35) __ run as other animals do. It moves hopping on its hind legs. They are much longer __

34.
    (A) if   (B) or
    (C) but   (D) and

35.
    (A) or   (B) and
    (C) but   (D) because

—Darken Your Choice with HB Pencil—

1.	(A) (B) (C) (D)	8.	(A) (B) (C) (D)	15.	(A) (B) (C) (D)	22	(A) (B) (C) (D)	29.	(A) (B) (C) (D)
2.	(A) (B) (C) (D)	9.	(A) (B) (C) (D)	16.	(A) (B) (C) (D)	23.	(A) (B) (C) (D)	30.	(A) (B) (C) (D)
3.	(A) (B) (C) (D)	10.	(A) (B) (C) (D)	17.	(A) (B) (C) (D)	24.	(A) (B) (C) (D)	31.	(A) (B) (C) (D)
4.	(A) (B) (C) (D)	11.	(A) (B) (C) (D)	18.	(A) (B) (C) (D)	25.	(A) (B) (C) (D)	32.	(A) (B) (C) (D)
5.	(A) (B) (C) (D)	12.	(A) (B) (C) (D)	19.	(A) (B) (C) (D)	26.	(A) (B) (C) (D)	33.	(A) (B) (C) (D)
6.	(A) (B) (C) (D)	13.	(A) (B) (C) (D)	20.	(A) (B) (C) (D)	27.	(A) (B) (C) (D)	34.	(A) (B) (C) (D)
7.	(A) (B) (C) (D)	14.	(A) (B) (C) (D)	21.	(A) (B) (C) (D)	28.	(A) (B) (C) (D)	35.	(A) (B) (C) (D)

ARTICLES AND PREPOSITIONS

LEARNING OBJECTIVES

➤ Articles and their usage
➤ Different types of Prepositions used in English

MULTIPLE CHOICE QUESTIONS

I. Fill in the blanks with the correct option:

1. I need _____ pen. Do you have one?
   (A) a   (B) an
   (C) the   (D) none

2. _________ Daksh is living in Mumbai.
   (A) A   (B) An
   (C) The   (D) None

3. A river flows by my house in the hills. _______ river is magnificent.
   (A) A   (B) An
   (C) The   (D) None

4. Do you need _________ umbrella?
   (A) a   (B) an
   (C) the   (D) none

5. Have you read _________ Bhagvad Gita?
   (A) a   (B) an
   (C) the   (D) none

6. _________ Eid is celebrated with a lot of love.
   (A) A
   (B) An
   (C) The
   (D) None

7. He offered me _________ apple to eat.
   (A) a   (B) an
   (C) the   (D) none

8. Have you ever seen _________ ostrich?
   (A) a   (B) an
   (C) the   (D) none

9. _________ volcano is located in the eastern corner of _________ city.
   (A) A, the   (B) An, a
   (C) The, the   (D) The, a

10. My mother is having _______ headache.
    (A) a   (B) an
    (C) the   (D) none

II. Complete the following:

11. _________ easy task
    (A) A   (B) An
    (C) The   (D) None

12. _________ longest jump
    (A) A   (B) An
    (C) The   (D) None

13. _________ unhappy unicorn
    (A) A   (B) An
    (C) The   (D) None

14. _______ hour later
    (A) A   (B) An
    (C) The   (D) None

15. _______ steepest mountain
    (A) A   (B) An
    (C) The   (D) None

I. **Choose the most suitable preposition to fill in the blanks:**

16. I met him two days _________ at the park.
    (A) in
    (B) towards
    (C) ago
    (D) below

17. I will meet you ____ the McDonald's outlet _______ 7 pm today.
    (A) in, below
    (B) at, above
    (C) across, at
    (D) at, At

18. We all went to that school _______ 2010.
    (A) till
    (B) by
    (C) below
    (D) ago

19. The little puppy was hiding _______ the car.
    (A) across
    (B) till
    (C) at
    (D) under

20. When I saw her at the mall, I waved at her and she started walking __________ me.
    (A) at
    (B) towards
    (C) by
    (D) below

21. We watched the movie _______ the living room.
    (A) across
    (B) by
    (C) till
    (D) in

22. I have not met my aunt _______ last Tuesday.
    (A) since
    (B) till
    (C) by
    (D) ago

23. We need to be _________ the theatre by 3 p.m. or we will miss the movie.
    (A) till
    (B) by
    (C) at
    (D) since

24. Rohit came to Delhi _______ the 15th of this month.
    (A) on
    (B) at
    (C) by
    (D) from

25. They were on the beach _______ 12 pm ______ 6 pm.
    (A) by, till
    (B) to, from
    (C) across, by
    (D) from, till

26. He is staying with us at least __________ Tuesday.
    (A) till
    (B) by
    (C) to
    (D) below

27. I waited for him for about half an hour __________ the staircase.
    (A) across
    (B) below
    (C) under
    (D) from

28. Astha's sister is getting married __________ the 27th of November.
    (A) by   (B) till
    (C) at   (D) on

29. She came to visit me 5 days _______.
    (A) since   (B) by
    (C) ago   (D) in

30. Can you please put the toys back _______ the box?
    (A) till   (B) across
    (C) into   (D) to

Fill in the blanks with the correct choice:

31. Rohan bought himself _________ vanilla ice-cream. It was _______ ice candy.
(A) An, A (B) A, The
(C) A, An (D) The, A

32. _______ beggar who met us offered us ________ fruit.
(A) An, A (B) A, The
(C) A, An (D) The, A

33. Sanil's pet was ________ eagle. ______ eagle was friendly.

(A) An, The (B) A, The
(C) A, An (D) The, A

Pick the correct preposition from the options and fill in the blanks:

34. Tarun placed the utensils ______ the sink.
(A) Over (B) Under
(C) Towards (D) In

35. The car arrived ________ the flight had landed.
(A) After (B) During
(C) Under (D) With

—Darken Your Choice with HB Pencil—

1.	Ⓐ Ⓑ Ⓒ Ⓓ	8.	Ⓐ Ⓑ Ⓒ Ⓓ	15.	Ⓐ Ⓑ Ⓒ Ⓓ	22	Ⓐ Ⓑ Ⓒ Ⓓ	29.	Ⓐ Ⓑ Ⓒ Ⓓ
2.	Ⓐ Ⓑ Ⓒ Ⓓ	9.	Ⓐ Ⓑ Ⓒ Ⓓ	16.	Ⓐ Ⓑ Ⓒ Ⓓ	23.	Ⓐ Ⓑ Ⓒ Ⓓ	30.	Ⓐ Ⓑ Ⓒ Ⓓ
3.	Ⓐ Ⓑ Ⓒ Ⓓ	10.	Ⓐ Ⓑ Ⓒ Ⓓ	17.	Ⓐ Ⓑ Ⓒ Ⓓ	24.	Ⓐ Ⓑ Ⓒ Ⓓ	31.	Ⓐ Ⓑ Ⓒ Ⓓ
4.	Ⓐ Ⓑ Ⓒ Ⓓ	11.	Ⓐ Ⓑ Ⓒ Ⓓ	18.	Ⓐ Ⓑ Ⓒ Ⓓ	25.	Ⓐ Ⓑ Ⓒ Ⓓ	32.	Ⓐ Ⓑ Ⓒ Ⓓ
5.	Ⓐ Ⓑ Ⓒ Ⓓ	12.	Ⓐ Ⓑ Ⓒ Ⓓ	19.	Ⓐ Ⓑ Ⓒ Ⓓ	26.	Ⓐ Ⓑ Ⓒ Ⓓ	33.	Ⓐ Ⓑ Ⓒ Ⓓ
6.	Ⓐ Ⓑ Ⓒ Ⓓ	13.	Ⓐ Ⓑ Ⓒ Ⓓ	20.	Ⓐ Ⓑ Ⓒ Ⓓ	27.	Ⓐ Ⓑ Ⓒ Ⓓ	34.	Ⓐ Ⓑ Ⓒ Ⓓ
7.	Ⓐ Ⓑ Ⓒ Ⓓ	14.	Ⓐ Ⓑ Ⓒ Ⓓ	21.	Ⓐ Ⓑ Ⓒ Ⓓ	28.	Ⓐ Ⓑ Ⓒ Ⓓ	35.	Ⓐ Ⓑ Ⓒ Ⓓ

SIMPLE TENSES

LEARNING OBJECTIVES

➤ Usage of simple tenses in English

MULTIPLE CHOICE QUESTIONS

I. Change the verb given in brackets into the correct form.

1. Every afternoon I (go) _________________ to the park.

2. It does (not/rain) _____________ here a lot.

3. We (see) ___________ some beautiful gardens in Jaipur last month.

4. I like to (eat) _________ at Chinese restaurants.

5. Ashley (see) _____________ this movie with me tomorrow.

6. The colour of this jacket (be) ___________ absolutely fine.

7. Mother (leave) _________ her shawl here when she left last week.

8. Next week I (go) _________ to Shimla for a holiday.

9. This park is best to (play) _____________ in the evenings.

10. I think she liked the cake. She (eat) _____________ at least half of it!

11. Amit (drive) _____________ his car last night.

12. Preeti and Sabina always (drink) ___________ tea. They are not fond of coffee.

13. Last Friday, her father (come) _____________ to drop her to the airport.

14. He _______________ (not/like) the food at the party two days ago.

15. Why don't you guys go ahead. I (late) __________ by another half an hour.

II. Choose the correct option from the ones given below.

16. I _______________ the video game all evening yesterday.
    (A) playing   (B) will play
    (C) played   (D) play

17. I __________ the taste of orange drink. I never drink it.
    (A) hate   (B) hated
    (C) will hate   (D) hating

18. Amrit ___________ something special. His mother is coming to visit him tonight.
    (A) cooked
    (B) cooking
    (C) will cook
    (D) cook

19. It's his birthday tomorrow, we __________ at 12 at night.
   (A) meeting   (B) met
   (C) meets   (D) will meet

20. The movie we __________ yesterday was too funny!
   (A) will watch   (B) watched
   (C) watch   (D) watching

21. She is very quick on the computer. She __________ this document in just half an hour once she reaches here.
   (A) type
   (B) typing
   (C) will type
   (D) has been typing

22. India __________ Pakistan by 150 runs last week.
   (A) defeats
   (B) will defeat
   (C) have been defeating
   (D) defeated

23. As a habit, she still __________ up every morning at 5 to go for a run.
   (A) waking
   (B) wakes
   (c) woken
   (d) wake

24. The hero in the movie always knows how to __________ and dance.
   (A) sings   (B) sang
   (C) singing   (D) sing

25. I __________ for you for only ten minutes more. Then I will leave.
   (A) will wait   (B) waited
   (C) waits   (D) waiting

26. Ashish __________ how to use this software vey well. He does it all the time.
   (A) knowing   (B) knows
   (C) know   (D) will know

27. Last Thursday, we __________ out for ice cream.
   (A) go   (B) going
   (C) went   (D) will go

28. His phone is out of reach but I __________ once again.
   (A) trying   (B) try
   (C) tried   (D) will try

29. I __________ her if she wanted some more water but she said no.
   (A) ask   (B) asked
   (C) will ask   (D) asking

30. Nowadays, we __________ this programme on TV every night.
   (A) watch   (B) watching
   (C) watched   (D) will watch

HOTS (ACHIEVERS SECTION)

Pick the option that fits the underlined phrases from the given alternatives:

31. We <u>are answering</u> question number one. We <u>will finish</u> it soon.
   (A) Simple Present Tense, Simple Past Tense
   (B) Future Continuous Tense, Present Continuous Tense
   (C) Present Continuous Tense, Simple Future Tense
   (D) Past Continuous Tense, Simple Future Tense

32. Geeta <u>ate</u> her lunch. She <u>eats</u> at one o'clock every day.
   (A) Simple Past Tense, Simple Present Tense
   (B) Future Continuous Tense, Present Continuous Tense
   (C) Present Continuous Tense, Simple Future Tense
   (D) Past Continuous Tense, Simple Future Tense

33. The boy <u>was playing</u> a board game. He <u>will be going</u> to bed soon.
   (A) Simple Past Tense, Simple Present Tense

(B) Future Continuous Tense, Present Continuous Tense

(C) Present Continuous Tense, Simple Future Tense

(D) Past Continuous Tense, Future Continuous Tense

34. I <u>will wash</u> my hands later. I <u>wash</u> them every evening.

(A) Simple Past Tense, Simple Present Tense

(B) Simple Future Tense, Simple Present Tense

(C) Present Continuous Tense, Simple Future Tense

(D) Past Continuous Tense, Simple Future Tense

35. Nikita <u>will be jumping</u> for joy soon. Her pet dog <u>recovered</u> from its illness.

(A) Simple Past Tense, Simple Present Tense

(B) Future Continuous Tense, Present Continuous Tense

(C) Present Continuous Tense, Simple Future Tense

(D) Future Continuous Tense, Simple Past Tense

1.	Ⓐ Ⓑ Ⓒ Ⓓ	8.	Ⓐ Ⓑ Ⓒ Ⓓ	15.	Ⓐ Ⓑ Ⓒ Ⓓ	22	Ⓐ Ⓑ Ⓒ Ⓓ	29.	Ⓐ Ⓑ Ⓒ Ⓓ
2.	Ⓐ Ⓑ Ⓒ Ⓓ	9.	Ⓐ Ⓑ Ⓒ Ⓓ	16.	Ⓐ Ⓑ Ⓒ Ⓓ	23.	Ⓐ Ⓑ Ⓒ Ⓓ	30.	Ⓐ Ⓑ Ⓒ Ⓓ
3.	Ⓐ Ⓑ Ⓒ Ⓓ	10.	Ⓐ Ⓑ Ⓒ Ⓓ	17.	Ⓐ Ⓑ Ⓒ Ⓓ	24.	Ⓐ Ⓑ Ⓒ Ⓓ	31.	Ⓐ Ⓑ Ⓒ Ⓓ
4.	Ⓐ Ⓑ Ⓒ Ⓓ	11.	Ⓐ Ⓑ Ⓒ Ⓓ	18.	Ⓐ Ⓑ Ⓒ Ⓓ	25.	Ⓐ Ⓑ Ⓒ Ⓓ	32.	Ⓐ Ⓑ Ⓒ Ⓓ
5.	Ⓐ Ⓑ Ⓒ Ⓓ	12.	Ⓐ Ⓑ Ⓒ Ⓓ	19.	Ⓐ Ⓑ Ⓒ Ⓓ	26.	Ⓐ Ⓑ Ⓒ Ⓓ	33.	Ⓐ Ⓑ Ⓒ Ⓓ
6.	Ⓐ Ⓑ Ⓒ Ⓓ	13.	Ⓐ Ⓑ Ⓒ Ⓓ	20.	Ⓐ Ⓑ Ⓒ Ⓓ	27.	Ⓐ Ⓑ Ⓒ Ⓓ	34.	Ⓐ Ⓑ Ⓒ Ⓓ
7.	Ⓐ Ⓑ Ⓒ Ⓓ	14.	Ⓐ Ⓑ Ⓒ Ⓓ	21.	Ⓐ Ⓑ Ⓒ Ⓓ	28.	Ⓐ Ⓑ Ⓒ Ⓓ	35.	Ⓐ Ⓑ Ⓒ Ⓓ

LEARNING OBJECTIVES

➤ Questions

➤ Question Tags

PRACTICE EXERCISE

Question 1 to 6: Fill in the blanks with the most suitable question words:

1. _________ much does this car cost?
   (A) When   (B) Which
   (C) How   (D) Whom

2. _________ did the flight arrive?
   (A) Which   (B) When
   (C) What   (D) Who

3. _________ of these shirts do you like?
   (A) Which   (B) Why
   (C) What   (D) Where

4. _______ will the summer vacations begin?
   (A) When   (B) Where
   (C) How   (D) Why

5. _________ is the baby crying?
   (A) When   (B) Who
   (C) Why   (D) Whom

Question 6 to 15 : Complete the sentences with the correct question tags:

6. She is collecting stickers, _________?
   (A) Isn't she
   (B) is she
   (C) she is not
   (D) she it is

7. Peter played handball yesterday, _________?
   (A) he did
   (B) didn't he
   (C) he did not
   (D) did he

8. Kevin will come tonight, _________?
   (A) won't he   (B) he won't
   (C) he will   (D) will he

9. The trip is very expensive, _________?
   (A) it is not   (B) it isn't
   (C) isn't it   (D) it is

10. There isn't an ATM _________?
    (A) is there   (B) isn't there
    (C) these is   (D) these isn't

11. They aren't in Mumbai at the moment _________?
    (A) are they   (B) they are
    (C) aren't they   (D) they are not

12. You aren't from Brazil, _________?
    (A) are you   (B) you are
    (C) aren't you   (D) you are not

13. I often come home late, _________?
    (A) I do not   (B) doesn't I
    (C) I does not   (D) don't I

14. Kiki doesn't write a letter before bed, _________?
    (A) does she
    (B) she does
    (C) she does not
    (D) doesn't she

15. Lucy will buy the dress, _________?
    (A) will she
    (B) she will
    (C) won't she
    (D) she won't

Question 16 to 19 : Change the following sentences into suitable questions:

16. I am going to Allahabad tomorrow.
    (A) How you are going to Allahabad?
    (B) Why are you going to Allahabad?
    (C) When are you going to Allahabad?
    (D) Are you going tomorrow?

17. We could do this work next month.
    (a) Could we do this work next month?
    (B) We could do this work when?
    (C) What is in next month?
    (D) None of the above.

18. It is 10:00 PM now.
    (A) It is what time?
    (B) What time is it now?
    (C) How is the time now?
    (D) None of the above.

19. I got to the station on a rickshaw.
    (A) How did you get the rickshaw?
    (B) How you got to the station?
    (C) How did you get to the station?
    (D) When did you get to the station?

1.	Ⓐ	Ⓑ	Ⓒ	Ⓓ	5.	Ⓐ	Ⓑ	Ⓒ	Ⓓ	9.	Ⓐ	Ⓑ	Ⓒ	Ⓓ	13	Ⓐ Ⓑ Ⓒ Ⓓ	17.	Ⓐ Ⓑ Ⓒ Ⓓ	
2.	Ⓐ	Ⓑ	Ⓒ	Ⓓ	6.	Ⓐ	Ⓑ	Ⓒ	Ⓓ	10.	Ⓐ	Ⓑ	Ⓒ	Ⓓ	14.	Ⓐ Ⓑ Ⓒ Ⓓ	18.	Ⓐ Ⓑ Ⓒ Ⓓ	
3.	Ⓐ	Ⓑ	Ⓒ	Ⓓ	7.	Ⓐ	Ⓑ	Ⓒ	Ⓓ	11.	Ⓐ	Ⓑ	Ⓒ	Ⓓ	15.	Ⓐ Ⓑ Ⓒ Ⓓ	19.	Ⓐ Ⓑ Ⓒ Ⓓ	
4.	Ⓐ	Ⓑ	Ⓒ	Ⓓ	8.	Ⓐ	Ⓑ	Ⓒ	Ⓓ	12.	Ⓐ	Ⓑ	Ⓒ	Ⓓ	16.	Ⓐ Ⓑ Ⓒ Ⓓ			

JUMBLED WORDS AND SENTENCES

LEARNING OBJECTIVES

➤ Concept of jumbled word and sentences

PRACTICE EXERCISE

Direction for Question 1 to 10: Arrange the letters to form meaningful words.

1. SINTA
    (A) Tinas   (B) Sinat
    (C) Saint   (D) Siant
2. LAVLEY
    (A) Vellay   (B) Levaly
    (C) Vaelly   (D) Valley
3. NCESIEC
    (A) Niececs   (B) Sceinec
    (C) Scemce   (D) Science
4. CSPEFICI
    (A) Speficic   (B) Specific
    (C) Spicefic   (D) Spicifec
5. SFERAELS
    (A) Fareless   (B) Faerless
    (C) Fearless   (D) Feraless
6. DGERAR
    (A) Regard   (B) Reagrd
    (C) Dregar   (D) Regadr
7. SKNA
    (A) Knas   (B) Naks
    (C) Skan   (D) Sank
8. RSPTEIS
    (A) Stripes
    (B) Trispes
    (C) Spriets
    (D) Priesst
9. HTSOI
    (A) Hosit   (B) Tosih
    (C) Hoist   (D) Toish
10. EONRW
    (A) Renow   (B) Woren
    (C) Wroen   (D) Owner

11. **Direction:** In each question four sentences are given. Identify the sentences among them which has words in the correct order,
    (A) Pets make great birds.
    (B) Great birds make pers.
    (C) Birds make great pets.
    (D) Great pets make birds.

12. **Direction:** In each question four sentences are given. Identify the sentences among them which has words in the correct order,
    (A) There is enough for us food.
    (B) Food is there enough for us.
    (C) Food is enough there for us.
    (D) There is enough food for us.

13. **Direction:** In each question four sentences are given. Identify the sentences among them which has words in the correct order,

(A) He had grown so big.
(B) He had big so grown.
(C) So he had big grown.
(D) So had he big grown.

14. **Direction:** In each question four sentences are given. Identify the sentences among them which has words in the correct order,
(A) The shone sun so beautifully.
(B) The sun shone so beautifully.
(C) The sun beautifully shone so.
(D) The shone so beautifully sun.

15. **Direction:** In each question four sentences are given. Identify the sentences among them which has words in the correct order,
(A) The little prince was frightened.
(B) The prince little was frightened.
(C) The frightened little was prince.
(D) The frightened prince was little.

16. **Direction:** In each question four sentences are given. Identify the sentences among them which has words in the correct order,
(A) He had a large collection of stamps.
(B) Large had a he collection of stamps.
(C) Stamps he had a large collection of.
(D) He had stamps a of large collection.

17. **Direction:** In each question four sentences are given. Identify the sentences among them which has words in the correct order,
(A) He travelled over all to China.
(B) He travelled all over to China.
(C) He travelled over to all China.
(D) He over travelled to all China.

18. **Direction:** In each question four sentences are given. Identify the sentences among them which has words in the correct order,

(A) They came across dark a house and that looked empty.
(B) They across came a dark and house that looked empty.
(C) A house came across they that looked empty and dark.
(D) They came across a house that looked dark and empty.

19. **Direction:** In each question four sentences are given. Identify the sentences among them which has words in the correct order,
(A) The king had everything he wanted.
(B) Everything he wanted had the king.
(C) He wanted everything had the king.
(D) The he king had everything wanted.

20. **Direction:** In each question four sentences are given. Identify the sentences among them which has words in the correct order,
(A) All the ships had returned except one.
(B) Ships had all the returned except one.
(C) All the returned ships had except one.
(D) Except one ships the all had returned.

21. **Direction:** In each question four words are given. You have to identify the word among them which does not have the letters in the correct order.
(A) Blanket
(B) Ceraels
(C) Precious
(D) Captain

22. **Direction:** In each question four words are given. You have to identify the word among them which does not have the letters in the correct order.
(A) Raom
(B) Valuable
(C) Great
(D) Appearances

23. **Direction:** In each question four words are given. You have to identify the word among them which does not have the letters in the correct order.
    (A) Compare
    (B) Bear
    (C) Nobel
    (D) Convenient

24. **Direction:** In each question four words are given. You have to identify the word among them which does not have the letters in the correct order.
    (A) Monument
    (B) Memory
    (C) Weight
    (D) Fecht
    (E) None of these

25. **Direction:** In each question four words are given. You have to identify the word among them which does not have the letters in the correct order.
    (A) Always
    (B) Refuse
    (C) Enouhg
    (D) Field

26. **Direction:** In each question four words are given. You have to identify the word among them which does not have the letters in the correct order.
    (A) Ripe
    (B) Obedeint
    (C) Guess
    (D) Courage

27. **Direction:** In each question four words are given. You have to identify the word among them which does not have the letters in the correct order.
    (A) Mention
    (B) Behave
    (C) Appreciate
    (D) Tear

28. **Direction:** In each question four words are given. You have to identify the word among them which does not have the letters in the correct order.
    (A) Crowd
    (B) Thworn
    (C) Trader
    (D) Produce

29. **Direction:** In each question four words are given. You have to identify the word among them which does not have the letters in the correct order.
    (A) Lesson
    (B) Laziness
    (C) Nowt
    (D) Farmer

30. **Direction:** In each question four words are given. You have to identify the word among them which does not have the letters in the correct order.
    (A) Perpare
    (B) Reward
    (C) Beat
    (D) Reason

31. **Direction:** Arrange P, Q, R and S to form meaningful sentences,
    P: the man Q: the R: truth S: was telling
    (A) PQRS   (B) PSQR
    (C) PRSQ   (D) PQSR
    (E) None of these

32. **Direction:** Arrange P, Q, R and S to form meaningful sentences,
    P: came Q: they R: across a S: great storm
    (A) QSRP   (B) PQSR
    (C) QPRS   (D) PRSQ

33. **Direction:** Arrange P, Q, R and S to form meaningful sentences,
    P: very good Q: they are R: friends of S: mine
    (A) QPRS   (B) QRSP
    (C) RSQP   (D) RQPS

34. **Direction:** Arrange P, Q, R and S to form meaningful sentences,
    P: this worked Q: for a R: very well S: time
    (A) PQSR
    (B) PQRS
    (C) QRSP
    (D) PROS

35. **Direction:** Arrange P, Q, R and S to form meaningful sentences,
    P: quick Q: I need R: bath S: to have a
    (A) QSPR
    (B) QRSP
    (C) PQSR
    (D) PRSQ

Darken Your Choice with HB Pencil

1.	Ⓐ Ⓑ Ⓒ Ⓓ	8.	Ⓐ Ⓑ Ⓒ Ⓓ	15.	Ⓐ Ⓑ Ⓒ Ⓓ	22	Ⓐ Ⓑ Ⓒ Ⓓ	29.	Ⓐ Ⓑ Ⓒ Ⓓ
2.	Ⓐ Ⓑ Ⓒ Ⓓ	9.	Ⓐ Ⓑ Ⓒ Ⓓ	16.	Ⓐ Ⓑ Ⓒ Ⓓ	23.	Ⓐ Ⓑ Ⓒ Ⓓ	30.	Ⓐ Ⓑ Ⓒ Ⓓ
3.	Ⓐ Ⓑ Ⓒ Ⓓ	10.	Ⓐ Ⓑ Ⓒ Ⓓ	17.	Ⓐ Ⓑ Ⓒ Ⓓ	24.	Ⓐ Ⓑ Ⓒ Ⓓ	31.	Ⓐ Ⓑ Ⓒ Ⓓ
4.	Ⓐ Ⓑ Ⓒ Ⓓ	11.	Ⓐ Ⓑ Ⓒ Ⓓ	18.	Ⓐ Ⓑ Ⓒ Ⓓ	25.	Ⓐ Ⓑ Ⓒ Ⓓ	32.	Ⓐ Ⓑ Ⓒ Ⓓ
5.	Ⓐ Ⓑ Ⓒ Ⓓ	12.	Ⓐ Ⓑ Ⓒ Ⓓ	19.	Ⓐ Ⓑ Ⓒ Ⓓ	26.	Ⓐ Ⓑ Ⓒ Ⓓ	33.	Ⓐ Ⓑ Ⓒ Ⓓ
6.	Ⓐ Ⓑ Ⓒ Ⓓ	13.	Ⓐ Ⓑ Ⓒ Ⓓ	20.	Ⓐ Ⓑ Ⓒ Ⓓ	27.	Ⓐ Ⓑ Ⓒ Ⓓ	34.	Ⓐ Ⓑ Ⓒ Ⓓ
7.	Ⓐ Ⓑ Ⓒ Ⓓ	14.	Ⓐ Ⓑ Ⓒ Ⓓ	21.	Ⓐ Ⓑ Ⓒ Ⓓ	28.	Ⓐ Ⓑ Ⓒ Ⓓ	35.	Ⓐ Ⓑ Ⓒ Ⓓ

COMPREHENSION

PRACTICE EXERCISE

Comprehension 1

Read the passage below and answer the questions that follow:

Milo is a lion cub. He was born to Mr. Khalif, the lion. Mr. Khalif is the king of the jungle. Though they live in a comfortable den in the forest, Mr. Khalif takes Milo to camp in the dense forests. He wants to raise a brave lion. Milo is very friendly with the other animals. He plays ludo with his zebra friend, Abu. Milo often says that it is very difficult to win at the game with Abu. In the evening, Mrs. Khalif bakes delicious cakes for Abu and Milo. They sometimes camp together with Mr. Khalif. Abu often tells Mr. Khalif that he is a very good king of the jungle and that all animals love him.

1. Who is Milo?

   ____

2. What is the name of Milo's zebra friend?

   ____

3. Why does Mr. Khalif take Milo to camp in the dense forest?

   ____

4. Which game is Abu very good at playing?

   ____

5. What does Mrs. Khalif do for Milo and Abu?

   ____

6. What does Abu often tell Mr. Khalif?

Comprehension 2

Read the passage below and answer the questions that follow:

Once there was a car called Derbie. Derbie was the fastest car in town. It had a shiny red number plate and four black wheels that went round and round the whole town. Derbie was proud of its owner, Mr. Biswas. Mr. Biswas would take Derbie to the garage every Sunday. There, the mechanic would give Derbie a good wash and change its tyres, if there was a need. Derbie is very special to Mr. Biswas as it is his first car. It is the car in which Mr. Biswas had brought his newly born son to his home.

Now Mr. Biswas has grown old. His son has also brought a new car. But Mr. Biswas still takes Derbie to the town every Sunday. It is not the fastest car now, but the oldest. Sometimes, Mr. Biswas takes Mrs. Biswas for long rides in the car and they listen to old songs. Derbie is also old, but is still very proud of its owners and is very fond of them.

7. Who is the story about?

   ____

8. What was so special about Derbie?

   ____

9. Name the owner of Derbie.

   ____

10. What did the mechanic at the garage do for Derbie?

11. Why is Derbie so special to Mr. Biswas?

12. Where does Mr. Biswas take Derbie every Sunday?

Comprehension 3

Read the conversation below and answer the questions that follow.

(Kshitij and Zaira are talking to their drama teacher, Mrs. Sen.)

Mrs. Sen: Kshitij and Zaira, I am going to give you the responsibility of selecting a play for the school morning assembly.

Kshitij: Ma'am, how many actors do we have?

Mrs. Sen: We have at least ten actors.

Zaira: My mother can write a play. She is a playwright. May I take her help?

Mrs. Sen: You may, but only if she has time.

Zaira: She has been quite busy lately. What else should we do?

Mrs. Sen: You should visit the library and look for a book that has a collection of short plays.

Kshitij: Ma'am, what kind of a play should we select?

Mrs. Sen: I think you should select a comedy. We want everybody to have a good start to their day.

Zaira: Ma'am, can we enact a scene from a movie?

Mrs. Sen: It should not be a problem, but please choose with care.

Kshitij: I have just the idea. What about a scene from the Harry Potter movie?

Mrs. Sen: That is a wonderful idea, children. I can easily arrange for the costumes too. Let me discuss this with the drama club tomorrow. Thank you for your help.

Khistij and Zaira (together): My pleasure, Ma'am.

13. Who is Mrs. Sen?

14. What responsibility does Mrs. Sen give to Kshitij and Zaira?

15. What does Zaira's mother do?

16. Why does Mrs. Sen want Kshitij and Zaira to choose a comedy?

17. Which movie does Kshitij suggest they should play a scene from?

18. Who does Mrs. Sen want to discuss the idea with?

Comprehension 4

Ashima's brother, Bharat, called to say that he would be coming by the Rajdhani Express at 7.00 p.m. He needs their father to pick him up from the station. But Ashima has to leave for her tuition classes. So, she decides to leave a message for her father, Mr. Kapoor. Read the message below and answer the questions that follow:

Dad

Bharat called to say that he will reach the railway station around 7.00 p.m. He needs you to pick him up from the railway station. I am going for my Maths tuition class. I will be back by 7.30 p.m. The car keys are in the bottom drawer of your study desk. See you soon.

Ashima

19. How are Ashima and Bharat related?

20. Why did Bharat call home?

21. Which train is Bharat coming from?

____

22. Where is Ashima going?

____

23. When will Ashima be back?

____

24. Where are Mr. Kapoor's car keys?

____

Comprehension 5

Read the invitation below and answer the questions that follow:

Mrs. and Mr. Pablo
would like to invite you to the
marriage of their son
Federick Pablo
to
the daughter of Mrs. and Mr. Pinto
Sunita Pinto
on Saturday, 22nd June 2019
at 3.00 p.m. in the afternoon
at the Sacred Heart Church, Mapusa, Goa
Please join us in blessing the couple.
RSVP

25. What is the occasion of the invitation?

____

26. Name the couple who is getting married.

____

27. Whose son is getting married?

____

28. Whose daughter is getting married?

____

29. When is the marriage taking place?

____

30. What is the venue of the marriage?

____

1.	Ⓐ Ⓑ Ⓒ Ⓓ	7.	Ⓐ Ⓑ Ⓒ Ⓓ	13.	Ⓐ Ⓑ Ⓒ Ⓓ	19	Ⓐ Ⓑ Ⓒ Ⓓ	25.	Ⓐ Ⓑ Ⓒ Ⓓ
2.	Ⓐ Ⓑ Ⓒ Ⓓ	8.	Ⓐ Ⓑ Ⓒ Ⓓ	14.	Ⓐ Ⓑ Ⓒ Ⓓ	20.	Ⓐ Ⓑ Ⓒ Ⓓ	26.	Ⓐ Ⓑ Ⓒ Ⓓ
3.	Ⓐ Ⓑ Ⓒ Ⓓ	9.	Ⓐ Ⓑ Ⓒ Ⓓ	15.	Ⓐ Ⓑ Ⓒ Ⓓ	21.	Ⓐ Ⓑ Ⓒ Ⓓ	27.	Ⓐ Ⓑ Ⓒ Ⓓ
4.	Ⓐ Ⓑ Ⓒ Ⓓ	10.	Ⓐ Ⓑ Ⓒ Ⓓ	16.	Ⓐ Ⓑ Ⓒ Ⓓ	22.	Ⓐ Ⓑ Ⓒ Ⓓ	28.	Ⓐ Ⓑ Ⓒ Ⓓ
5.	Ⓐ Ⓑ Ⓒ Ⓓ	11.	Ⓐ Ⓑ Ⓒ Ⓓ	17.	Ⓐ Ⓑ Ⓒ Ⓓ	23.	Ⓐ Ⓑ Ⓒ Ⓓ	29.	Ⓐ Ⓑ Ⓒ Ⓓ
6.	Ⓐ Ⓑ Ⓒ Ⓓ	12.	Ⓐ Ⓑ Ⓒ Ⓓ	18.	Ⓐ Ⓑ Ⓒ Ⓓ	24.	Ⓐ Ⓑ Ⓒ Ⓓ	30.	Ⓐ Ⓑ Ⓒ Ⓓ

SPOKEN AND WRITTTEN EXPRESSION; PUNCTUATION

LEARNING OBJECTIVES

➤ Spoken and Written Expression
➤ Punctuation

PRACTICE EXERCISE

I. Choose the correct alternative from the given options:

1. You wish someone in the morning by saying _______
    (A) Good evening
    (B) Good night
    (C) Good morning
    (D) Good bye

2. When you greet someone close to you, you say, _______ to them.
    (A) Here
    (B) Hello
    (C) Yo
    (D) Ok

3. What do you say when someone is leaving?
    (A) Good job
    (B) Good work
    (C) Good riddance
    (D) Good bye

4. How do you wish someone on their wedding anniversary?
    (A) Well done
    (B) Merry Wedding Anniversary
    (C) Get well soon
    (D) Happy Wedding Anniversary

5. What will you say when someone shares a piece of good news with you?
    (A) Get well soon
    (B) Congratulations
    (C) Happy birthday
    (D) Happy new year

6. What will you say to a person who is not well?
    (A) Get well soon
    (B) Congratulations
    (C) Happy birthday
    (D) Happy new year

7. How will you wish someone on Christmas?
    (A) Happy birthday
    (B) Merry Christmas
    (C) Happy new year
    (D) Happy Easter

8. Which of the following is the correct response to 'How do you do?'
    (A) Who are you?
    (B) My name is Peter.
    (C) Peter is very good.
    (D) I am fine. Thank you.

9. What do you say when you introduce yourself to a person for the first time?
    (A) Your thoughts about the weather.

(B) Your name and a little bit about yourself.

(C) Your address

(D) Your hobbies

10. Which of the following is the correct response to 'Nice to meet you'?

(A) You are wearing a nice scarf.

(B) I am fine, thank you.

(C) What is your name?

(D) Same here.

11. Which of the following expression shows gratitude?

(A) Congratulations

(B) Happy birthday

(C) Thank you

(D) Well done

12. Which of the following is a nice way of responding to a 'Thank you'?

(A) But why?

(B) Who are you?

(C) You are welcome.

(D) Really?

13. Which of the following expressions is used mostly while asking for permission?

(A) Please

(B) Sorry

(C) Thank you

(D) Well done

14. Which of the following expressions is used when someone gives you permission to do something?

(A) No, please don't.

(B) Please feel free.

(C) I am afraid, you can't.

(D) Thank you

15. Which of the following expressions is used when someone does not give you permission to do something?

(A) Yes, please do.

(B) I am afraid, you can't.

(C) Sure, go ahead.

(D) No problem.

II. Complete the following dialogues.

16. (Ravi and Vinod meet at the park. Vinod is with his wife.)

Ravi: Hello Vinod. How are you?

Vinod: a._____________, thank you. This is my wife, Nisha. And Nisha, this is Ravi, my colleague.

Ravi: Hello Nisha. b._____________ .

Nisha: Hello Ravi. Nice to meet you, too.

Ravi: I heard you two had a baby girl. c. _____________ .

Nisha and Vinod: d._____________ Ravi.

Ravi: Have you chosen a name for the baby yet?

Nisha: We haven't decided yet. But we are having a ceremony for the baby tomorrow. I hope Vinod has invited you.

Ravi: Of course, I will come. I must leave now. e. _____________ .

Nisha and Vinod: Yes, see you soon.

17. (Rahul and Arti are meeting for the first time.)

Rahul: Good morning. I am a. _______.

Arti: Good morning Rahul. I am Arti. Pleased to meet you.

Rahul: b._____________ too. I want to know about the book that you are writing.

Arti: It is nearly done. But I am finding it difficult to conclude the book. Do you know of a good library where I can find some classics?

Rahul: Oh yes, there is a library right next to my house. c. _______ give me a list of the books that you need. I will get them for you.

Arti: d._______ Rahul. I appreciate it.

Rahul: e._______, no problem.

18. **(Ritu needs her mother's permission to go to watch a movie with her friends.)**

Ritu: Mom, my friends are going to watch the new movie that has released this Friday. a.________ I go with them?

Mother: b. ______________, you can't go. We have guests over.

Ritu: c. ____________ okay if I go next weekend?

Mother: d. _________, please do.

Ritu: e. ____________ so much, mom.

MODEL TEST PAPER

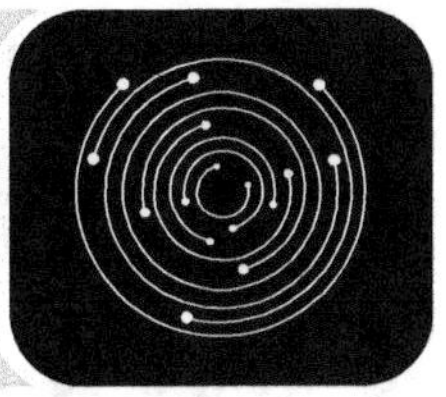

PRACTICE EXERCISE

SECTION I: Word and Structure Knowledge

Directions (1 – 5): Choose the correct sound of the given word from the options.

1. Bee
   (A) Beezzz   (B) Bizz
   (C) Buzz   (D) Buesss

2. Lion
   (A) Roar   (B) Grrrrr
   (C) Snarl   (D) Growl

3. Duck
   (A) Moo   (B) Cackle
   (C) Honk   (D) Quack

4. Seal
   (A) Barks   (B) Yips
   (C) Chatters   (D) Giggles

5. Whale
   (A) Gurgles   (B) Talks
   (C) Wails   (D) Sings

Directions (6 – 10): Find the odd word.

6. (A) Book   (B) Leaf
   (C) Scale   (D) Eraser

7. (A) Banana   (B) Cheese
   (C) Cherry   (D) Mango

8. (A) Feet   (B) Fingers
   (C) Palm   (D) Hand

9. (A) Happy   (B) Joyful
   (C) Gloomy   (D) Cheerful

10. (A) Uniform   (B) Badge
    (C) Bag   (D) Sandwich

Directions (11–14): Make a proper word from the spellings and find out the correct option.

11. Coltionlec
    (A) Tioncollec
    (B) Collection
    (C) Tioncocell
    (D) Cellcotion

12. Refnceere
    (A) Reference   (B) Encerrefe
    (C) Renceefe   (D) Fererence

13. Mediateim
    (A) Diateemim   (B) Immediate
    (C) Mimetedia   (D) Tedimemia

14. Sionadmis
    (A) Dionamiss   (B) Missadion
    (C) Admission   (D) Amisdsion

Directions (15–20): Select the right word to fit the description.

15. My fingers are __________ after writing the exam.
    (A) Sweating
    (B) Swelling
    (C) Itching
    (D) Cramping

16. Use a dictionary to look ______ these words.
    (A) Down   (B) See
    (C) Through   (D) Up

17. The hole was big enough to look _______.
    (A) At   (B) Through
    (C) In   (D) Out

18. Police have warned the local residents to be on the look-out for the prisoner who had __________.
    (A) Escaped   (B) Scary
    (C) Happy   (D) Loose
19. Keith was sitting all ________ himself.
    (A) From   (B) Next to
    (C) By   (D) Apart
20. There was a ________ bang.
    (A) Clear   (B) Noisy
    (C) Loud   (D) Sad

SECTION II: Reading

Sports days, sometimes referred to as field days, are events staged by many schools and offices in which people take part in competitive sporting activities, often with the aim of winning trophies or prizes. Though they are often held at the beginning of summer, they are also staged in the autumn or spring seasons, especially in countries where the summer is very harsh. Schools stage many sports days in which children participate in the sporting events. It is usually held in elementary schools, or grades Kindergarten-8th Grade.

In schools which use a house system, a feature of the school is the competition between the houses; this is especially brought out during sporting events such as an inter-house sports day.

Games that are played on school sports days can be wide and varied. They can include straightforward sprints and longer races for all age groups as well as egg and spoon races. Three legged races are run as well as sack races and parent and child races.

On the basis of the above paragraph, answer these questions.

21. What are field days known as?
    (A) Sports day
    (B) Match Day
    (C) House Day
    (D) Race Day

22. What does 'Competitive' mean?
    (A) Relating to computers
    (B) Relating to competition
    (C) To be spirited
    (D) To compute
23. What do the participants win after participating ?
    (A) Hugs
    (B) Cars
    (C) Money
    (D) Trophies or Prizes
24. Explain Inter-house Sports day.
    (A) Children from the same housing complex compete against others
    (B) Children run from one house to another
    (C) Schools who feature the house system make it an event for competition between the houses
    (D) Houses play sports
25. Do offices also have sports days?
    (A) I don't know
    (B) Yes
    (C) No
    (D) May be
26. Is Sports day only for children?
    (A) No
    (B) Yes
    (C) No, offices as well as parents partici-pate in some races
    (D) None of these
27. Which of these sports take place on Sports day?
    (A) Hurdles
    (B) Long jump
    (C) Hopping races
    (D) Long sprints and three legged races

SECTION III: Spoken and Written Expression
Directions (28 – 32): Choose the best reply to complete each conversation.

28. Zara: I think my laptop needs to be repaired
    Nicki:

(A) I'll give you the number of the repair shop I use.
(B) I can't help you.
(C) So fix it.
(D) None of these.

29. Tim: Hi, my name is Tim.
Peter:
(A) Hello
(B) Okay
(C) Hey, my name is Peter.
(D) None of these.

30. Nina: Do you need some help with the poster?
Teena:
(A) Yes, thank you for offering.
(B) I don't need your help.
(C) No, thanks.
(D) None of these.

31. Sourav: Oh no! I lost my pen.
Indu:
(A) Sorry, I can't help you.
(B) I'll help you search for it.
(C) It doesn't concern me.
(D) None of these.

32. Sara: How long is the flight to Mumbai?
Moni:
(A) It doesn't matter to me.
(B) Please don't ask me.
(C) Two and a half hours, if my estimation is correct.
(D) None of these.

Direction (33 – 35): Choose the best option to complete the passage.

33. Leela and Maya love to play 'Kitchen'. They spent the whole day pretending to cook fancy dishes. When they grow up they want to________.
(A) Live in a kitchen
(B) Become engineers
(C) Become chefs
(D) None of these

34. Meena loves her grandfather very much. His favourite activity is to paint. So, Meena gave some _______ to her grandfather for his birthday.
(A) Painting equipment
(B) A painting
(C) A brush
(D) None of these.

35. Ravi gets the highest marks in class. He _______ and is dedicated to his studies.
(A) Doesn't study
(B) Works hard
(C) Studies.
(D) None of these.

Darken Your Choice with HB Pencil

1.	(A) (B) (C) (D)	8.	(A) (B) (C) (D)	15.	(A) (B) (C) (D)	22	(A) (B) (C) (D)	29.	(A) (B) (C) (D)
2.	(A) (B) (C) (D)	9.	(A) (B) (C) (D)	16.	(A) (B) (C) (D)	23.	(A) (B) (C) (D)	30.	(A) (B) (C) (D)
3.	(A) (B) (C) (D)	10.	(A) (B) (C) (D)	17.	(A) (B) (C) (D)	24.	(A) (B) (C) (D)	31.	(A) (B) (C) (D)
4.	(A) (B) (C) (D)	11.	(A) (B) (C) (D)	18.	(A) (B) (C) (D)	25.	(A) (B) (C) (D)	32.	(A) (B) (C) (D)
5.	(A) (B) (C) (D)	12.	(A) (B) (C) (D)	19.	(A) (B) (C) (D)	26.	(A) (B) (C) (D)	33.	(A) (B) (C) (D)
6.	(A) (B) (C) (D)	13.	(A) (B) (C) (D)	20.	(A) (B) (C) (D)	27.	(A) (B) (C) (D)	34.	(A) (B) (C) (D)
7.	(A) (B) (C) (D)	14.	(A) (B) (C) (D)	21.	(A) (B) (C) (D)	28.	(A) (B) (C) (D)	35.	(A) (B) (C) (D)

HINTS AND SOLUTIONS

1. WORD POWER

Answer Key

1. (A)	2. (C)	3. (B)	4. (C)	5. (A)	6. (C)	7. (A)	8. (D)	9. (A)	10. (C)
11. (B)	12. (C)	13. (D)	14. (B)	15. (C)	16. (A)	17. (C)	18. (D)	19. (A)	20. (B)
21. (A)	22. (C)	23. (B)	24. (D)	25. (D)	26. (B)	27. (C)	28. (B)	29. (D)	30. (A)

HOTS (ACHIEVERS SECTION)

31. (C)	32. (D)	33. (A)	34. (D)	35. (C)

2. SYNONYMS AND ANTONYMS

Answer Key

1. (B)	2. (A)	3. (C)	4. (B)	5. (C)	6. (A)	7. (C)	8. (A)	9. (C)	10. (A)
11. (A)	12. (A)	13. (A)	14. (A)	15. (B)	16. (A)	17. (C)	18. (B)	19. (B)	20. (B)
21. (A)	22. (C)	23. (B)	24. (A)	25. (C)	26. (A)	27. (A)	28. (B)	29. (A)	30. (B)

HOTS (ACHIEVERS SECTION)

31. (A)	32. (C)	33. (D)	34. (A)	35. (D)

3. GENDER AND RELATIONS

Answer Key

1. (B)	2. (D)	3. (D)	4. (C)	5. (D)	6. (D)	7. (A)	8. (B)	9. (D)	10. (A)
11. (B)	12. (C)	13. (C)	14. (D)	15. (C)	16. (B)	17. (A)	18. (A)	19. (C)	20. (A)
21. (B)	22. (A)	23. (C)	24. (B)	25. (A)					

HOTS (ACHIEVERS SECTION)

26. (C)	27. (D)	28. (D)	29. (C)	30. (D)

Answer Key

1. (C)	2. (B)	3. (B)	4. (B)	5. (D)	6. (A)	7. (C)	8. (D)	9. (C)	10. (A)
11. (D)	12. (C)	13. (C)	14. (A)	15. (B)	16. (B)	17. (C)	18. (C)	19. (B)	20. (A)
21. (B)	22. (D)	23. (A)	24. (B)	25. (C)					

HOTS (ACHIEVERS SECTION)

26. (C)	27. (D)	28. (C)	29. (D)	30. (B)

5. PROVERBS AND IDIOMS

Answer Key

1. (C)	2. (C)	3. (A)	4. (C)	5. (A)	6. (C)	7. (C)	8. (A)	9. (D)	10. (A)
11. (B)	12. (C)	13. (D)	14. (B)	15. (C)	16. (C)	17. (A)	18. (D)	19. (A)	20. (C)

1. **(C)**

   Bear up means to show courage or determination during a difficult or unpleasant time, so does 'to put up with'. Hence other options are irrelevant.

2. **(C)**

   Take down and write are both synonyms of each other and can be replaced with each other. Others options are redundant.

3. **(A)**

   Bring forth or bring to light are the same in meaning. Other options do not conform to the phrase "bring forth'.

4. **(C)**

   Break down means 'failing in something and can be replaced with each other. Other options break into small pieces, beat up and enter a place do not correspond with the given phrase.

5. **(A)**

   Call for means demand for something. Hence it is the right option.

6. **(C)**

   Carry out means 'to execute something. 5o other options are not relevant.

7. **(C)**

   Give up means 'to stop doing something' and can easily be replaced with each other.

8. **(A)**

   Stand against means 'to object to something'

9. **(D)**

   Get off can be replaced with climb down. Example: You get off the bus or you climb down the bus.

10. **(A)**

    Go into and move inside are also the same in meaning. Hence can be replaced with each other.

11. **(B)**

    feeling blue means feeling sad.

12. **(C)**

    under the weather means feeling ill or sick.

13. **(D)**

cold shoulder means paying "no heed", or giving no attention.

14. (B)

down to earth means the person is simple and with no tantrums.

15. (C)

16. (C)

if you can't cut the mustard, you cannot deal with problems or difficulties.

17. (A)

go out on a limb means-to take a risk.

18. (D)

no dice is used when something that you say in order to refuse a request or to make clear that something is not possible.

19. (A)

hit the hay means prepare for sleep.

20. (C)

icing on the cake means an additional benefit to something already good.

HOTS (ACHIEVERS SECTION)

21. (C)	22. (B)	23. (B)	24. (D)	25. (A)

6. NOUNS AND PRONOUNS

Answer Key

1. (D)	2. (A)	3. (C)	4. (B)	5. (A)	6. (A)	7. (B)	8. (B)	9. (B)	10. (C)
11. (B)	12. (B)	13. (A)	14. (B)	15. (A)	16. (C)	17. (B)	18. (D)	19. (A)	20. (B)
21. (C)	22. (A)	23. (B)	24. (B)	25. (D)	26. (C)	27. (B)	28. (A)	29. (D)	30. (B)

HOTS (ACHIEVERS SECTION)

31. (B)	32. (A)	33. (C)	34. (A)	35. (D)

7. VERBS AND ADVERBS

Answer Key

1. (D)	2. (C)	3. (A)	4. (C)	5. (D)	6. (B)	7. (C)	8. (D)	9. (B)	10. (A)
11. (C)	12. (D)	13. (C)	14. (B)	15. (C)	16. (B)	17. (A)	18. (C)	19. (B)	20. (D)
21. (A)	22. (C)	23. (B)	24. (C)	25. (A)	26. (D)	27. (B)	28. (C)	29. (A)	30. (C)

HOTS (ACHIEVERS SECTION)

31. (B)	32. (C)	33. (C)	34. (B)	35. (A)

8. ADJECTIVE AND CONJUNCTIONS

Answer Key

1. (A)	2. (D)	3. (C)	4. (A)	5. (A)	6. (A)	7. (C)	8. (D)	9. (B)	10. (A)
11. (A)	12. (D)	13. (A)	14. (D)	15. (D)	16. (C)	17. (C)	18. (C)	19. (D)	20. (A)
21. (B)	22. (B)	23. (A)	24. (C)	25. (B)	26. (B)	27. (B)	28. (C)	29. (C)	30. (C)

HOTS (ACHIEVERS SECTION)

31. (A)	32. (B)	33. (C)	34. (C)	35. (A)

9. ARTICLES AND PREPOSITIONS

Answer Key

1. (A)	2. (D)	3. (C)	4. (B)	5. (C)	6. (D)	7. (B)	8. (B)	9. (C)	10. (A)
11. (B)	12. (C)	13. (B)	14. (B)	15. (C)	16. (C)	17. (D)	18. (A)	19. (D)	20. (B)
21. (D)	22. (A)	23. (C)	24. (A)	25. (D)	26. (A)	27. (C)	28. (D)	29. (C)	30. (C)

HOTS (ACHIEVERS SECTION)

31. (C)	32. (D)	33. (A)	34. (D)	35. (A)

10. SIMPLE TENSES

Answer Key

I

1. Go	2. Not rain	3. Saw	4. Eat	5. Will see
6. Is	7. Left	8. Will go	9. Play	10. Ate
11. Drove	12. Drink	13. Came	14. Did not like	15. Will be late

II

16. (C)	17. (A)	18. (C)	19. (D)	20. (B)	21. (C)	22. (D)	23. (B)	24. (D)	25. (A)

HOTS (ACHIEVERS SECTION)

26. (C)	27. (A)	28. (D)	29. (B)	30. (D)

11. QUESTION AND QUESTION TAGS

				Answer Key					
1. (C)	2. (B)	3. (A)	4. (A)	5. (C)	6. (A)	7. (B)	8. (A)	9. (C)	10. (A)
11. (A)	12. (A)	13. (D)	14. (A)	15. (C)					

HOTS (ACHIEVERS SECTION)				
16. (C)	17. (A)	18. (B)	19. (C)	

12. JUMBLED WORDS AND SENTENCES

				Answer Key					
1. (C)	2. (D)	3. (D)	4. (B)	5. (C)	6. (A)	7. (D)	8. (A)	9. (C)	10. (D)
11. (C)	12. (D)	13. (A)	14. (B)	15. (A)	16. (A)	17. (B)	18. (D)	19. (A)	20. (A)
21. (B)	22. (A)	23. (D)	24. (D)	25. (C)	26. (B)	27. (C)	28. (B)	29. (C)	30. (A)

HOTS (ACHIEVERS SECTION)				
31. (B)	32. (C)	33. (A)	34. (D)	35. (A)

13. COMPREHENSION

Answer Key
Comprehension 1
1. Milo is a lion cub.
2. The name of Milo's zebra friend is Abu.
3. Mr. Khalif takes Milo to camp in the dense forest because he wants to raise a brave lion.
4. Abu is very good at playing ludo.
5. Mrs. Khalif bakes delicious cakes for Abu and Milo.
6. Abu often tells Mr. Khalif that he is a very good king of the jungle and that all animals love him.
Comprehension 2
7. The story is about Derbie, a car.

8. Derbie was the fastest car in town.
9. Mr. Biswas is the owner of Derbie.
10. The mechanic at the garage would give Derbie a good wash and change its tyres, if there was a need.
11. Derbie is very special to Mr. Biswas as it is his first car. It is the car in which Mr. Biswas had brought his newly born son to his home.
12. Mr. Biswas takes Derbie to the town every Sunday.
Comprehension 3
13. Mrs. Sen is the drama teacher of Kshitij and Zaira.
14.   Mrs. Sen gives Kshitij and Zaira the responsibility of selecting a play for the school morning assembly.
15. Zaira's mother writes plays. She is a playwright.
16. Mrs. Sen wants Kshitij and Zaira to choose a comedy because she wants everybody to have a good start to their day.
17. Kshitij suggests that they should play a scene from the Harry Potter movie.
18. Mrs. Sen wants to discuss the idea with the drama club.
Comprehension 4
19. Ashima and Bharat are sister and brother.
20. Bharat called home to say that he needs their father to pick him up from the station.
21. Bharat is coming by the Rajdhani Express at 7.00 p.m.
22. Ashima is going for her Maths tuition class.
23. Ashima will be back by 7.30 p.m.
24. Mr Kapoor's car keys are in the bottom drawer of his study desk.
Comprehension 5
25. The occasion of the invitation is a marriage ceremony.
26. Federick Pablo and Sunita Pinto are getting married to each other.
27. Mrs. and Mr. Pablo's son is getting married.
28. Mrs. and Mr. Pinto's daughter is getting married.
29. The marriage is taking place on Saturday, 22nd June 2019.
30. The venue of the marriage is Sacred Heart Church, Mapusa, Goa.

Answer Key

1. (C)	2. (B)	3. (D)	4. (D)	5. (B)	6. (A)	7. (B)	8. (D)	9. (B)	10. (D)
11. (C)	12. (C)	13. (A)	14. (B)	15. (B)					
16. (a) I am fine	(b) Nice to meet you	(c) Congratulations		(d) Thank you		(e) See you later			
17. (a) Rahul	(b) Pleased to meet you	(c) Please		(d) Thank you		(e) Sure			
18. (a) May	(b) I am afraid	(c) Is it		(d) Yes		(e) Thank you			

MODEL TEST PAPER

Answer Key

1. (C)	2. (A)	3. (D)	4. (A)	5. (D)	6. (B)	7. (B)	8. (A)	9. (C)	10. (D)
11. (B)	12. (A)	13. (B)	14. (C)	15. (B)	16. (B)	17. (B)	18. (A)	19. (C)	20. (C)
21. (A)	22. (B)	23. (D)	24. (C)	25. (B)	26. (A)	27. (D)	28. (A)	29. (C)	30. (A)
31. (B)	32. (C)	33. (C)	34. (A)	35. (B)					

SAMPLE OMR ANSWER SHEET

1. STUDENT NAME (IN ENGLISH CAPITAL LETTERS ONLY)

Students must write and darken the respective circles completely using HB Pencil only. Othewise their Answer Sheets will not be evaluated.

PERSONAL DETAILS

2. SCHOOL CODE

3. CLASS

4. SECTION

5. ROLL NO.

6. QUESTION PAPER SET

A ○ B ○ C ○ D ○

7. MOBILE NUMBER

8. GENDER

MALE ○

FEMALE ○

9. STREAM
(Only for Class XI and XII Students)

MATHEMATICS ○
BIOLOGY ○
OTHERS ○

MARK YOUR ANSWERS

No.	A	B	C	D	No.	A	B	C	D
1.	Ⓐ	Ⓑ	Ⓒ	Ⓓ	26.	Ⓐ	Ⓑ	Ⓒ	Ⓓ
2.	Ⓐ	Ⓑ	Ⓒ	Ⓓ	27.	Ⓐ	Ⓑ	Ⓒ	Ⓓ
3.	Ⓐ	Ⓑ	Ⓒ	Ⓓ	28.	Ⓐ	Ⓑ	Ⓒ	Ⓓ
4.	Ⓐ	Ⓑ	Ⓒ	Ⓓ	29.	Ⓐ	Ⓑ	Ⓒ	Ⓓ
5.	Ⓐ	Ⓑ	Ⓒ	Ⓓ	30.	Ⓐ	Ⓑ	Ⓒ	Ⓓ
6.	Ⓐ	Ⓑ	Ⓒ	Ⓓ	31.	Ⓐ	Ⓑ	Ⓒ	Ⓓ
7.	Ⓐ	Ⓑ	Ⓒ	Ⓓ	32.	Ⓐ	Ⓑ	Ⓒ	Ⓓ
8.	Ⓐ	Ⓑ	Ⓒ	Ⓓ	33.	Ⓐ	Ⓑ	Ⓒ	Ⓓ
9.	Ⓐ	Ⓑ	Ⓒ	Ⓓ	34.	Ⓐ	Ⓑ	Ⓒ	Ⓓ
10.	Ⓐ	Ⓑ	Ⓒ	Ⓓ	35.	Ⓐ	Ⓑ	Ⓒ	Ⓓ
11.	Ⓐ	Ⓑ	Ⓒ	Ⓓ	36.	Ⓐ	Ⓑ	Ⓒ	Ⓓ
12.	Ⓐ	Ⓑ	Ⓒ	Ⓓ	37.	Ⓐ	Ⓑ	Ⓒ	Ⓓ
13.	Ⓐ	Ⓑ	Ⓒ	Ⓓ	38.	Ⓐ	Ⓑ	Ⓒ	Ⓓ
14.	Ⓐ	Ⓑ	Ⓒ	Ⓓ	39.	Ⓐ	Ⓑ	Ⓒ	Ⓓ
15.	Ⓐ	Ⓑ	Ⓒ	Ⓓ	40.	Ⓐ	Ⓑ	Ⓒ	Ⓓ
16.	Ⓐ	Ⓑ	Ⓒ	Ⓓ	41.	Ⓐ	Ⓑ	Ⓒ	Ⓓ
17.	Ⓐ	Ⓑ	Ⓒ	Ⓓ	42.	Ⓐ	Ⓑ	Ⓒ	Ⓓ
18.	Ⓐ	Ⓑ	Ⓒ	Ⓓ	43.	Ⓐ	Ⓑ	Ⓒ	Ⓓ
19.	Ⓐ	Ⓑ	Ⓒ	Ⓓ	44.	Ⓐ	Ⓑ	Ⓒ	Ⓓ
20.	Ⓐ	Ⓑ	Ⓒ	Ⓓ	45.	Ⓐ	Ⓑ	Ⓒ	Ⓓ
21.	Ⓐ	Ⓑ	Ⓒ	Ⓓ	46.	Ⓐ	Ⓑ	Ⓒ	Ⓓ
22.	Ⓐ	Ⓑ	Ⓒ	Ⓓ	47.	Ⓐ	Ⓑ	Ⓒ	Ⓓ
23.	Ⓐ	Ⓑ	Ⓒ	Ⓓ	48.	Ⓐ	Ⓑ	Ⓒ	Ⓓ
24.	Ⓐ	Ⓑ	Ⓒ	Ⓓ	49.	Ⓐ	Ⓑ	Ⓒ	Ⓓ
25.	Ⓐ	Ⓑ	Ⓒ	Ⓓ	50.	Ⓐ	Ⓑ	Ⓒ	Ⓓ

Signature of the Student & Date of Examination

Signature of the Invigilator & Date of Examination

V&S Publishers, F-2/16 Ansari Road, Daryaganj, New Delhi-110002, ☎ 011-23240026-27
✉ info@vspublishers.com, 🌐 www.vspublishers.com